I0895249

The Architectural Legacy of Wallace A. Rayfield

FOUNDER
OF THE FIRM
W·A·RAYFIELD & CO., ARCHITECTS
BIRMINGHAM, ALA.

The Architectural Legacy of Wallace A. Rayfield

Pioneer Black Architect of Birmingham, Alabama

Allen R. Durough

The University of Alabama Press
Tuscaloosa

The University of Alabama Press
Tuscaloosa, Alabama 35487-0380
uapress.ua.edu

Copyright © 2010 by Allen R. Durough
All rights reserved.

Inquiries about reproducing material from this work should be addressed to the University of Alabama Press.

Typeface: Granjon

Cover image: Sixteenth Baptist Church, Birmingham, Alabama
Cover design: Michele Myatt Quinn

Unless otherwise indicated in a credit line, all illustrations are from the author's collection, © by Allen R. Durough.

E-ISBN: 978-0-8173-9619-0

Cataloging-in-Publication data is available from the Library of Congress.
ISBN: 978-0-8173-1683-9

Contents

Illustrations

Preface

The Architectural Legacy of Wallace A. Rayfield evolved from a discovery of 411 printing plates previously belonging to Mr. Rayfield in October 1993, as I prepared to tear down an old barn on my property in Bessemer, Alabama. Age had taken its toll on the dilapidated structure and it was in danger of falling down. I had contracted to have a bulldozer come in and demolish the old building, but before the bulldozer came, Danny Boyd, a young Church of God minister from Brookwood, Alabama, stopped by to salvage lumber and tin from the barn. Being a Christian and an ordained Baptist minister myself, I felt led to grant his request. I told him that if he would sign a liability release and help me move the items stored in the barn to an adjacent building, I would let him salvage the lumber and tin.

As we emptied the old barn, which was quite elaborately designed, we reached the last room. The floor was rotten and hazardous. We could see a number of metal boxes stacked in the back corner. From a distance, they appeared to contain rubber stamps. Because the floor was so dangerous, I was inclined to leave them, but for some reason, perhaps God's eternal plan, Danny insisted on getting them out. As I stepped toward the boxes the floor gave way and one leg went through the floor, skinning my shin. I then became more determined to leave them, but Danny insisted on getting the boxes out. Since they were against an outside wall, Danny said he would go around the barn and pull off the outside boards. In the meantime I carefully made my way back to the boxes.

As I reached the boxes, I discovered they contained metal printing plates. However, I had no clue as to their true significance. When I examined them, I saw beautiful drawings of churches, schools, and other buildings. I saw business advertisements bearing the title of W. A. Rayfield & Co., Architects. There were also a few portraits in the mix. In addition, I saw on the tops of the metal boxes inscriptions such as "W. A. Rayfield Church Architect" and "W. A. Rayfield School Architect." Excitement began to build and my mind was spinning as I wondered about the significance of the old artifacts.

By that time Danny had opened a large hole in the side of the barn. Failing to realize the value of the artifacts, I began throw-

ing them out into the yard like Frisbees, putting a slight scratch on the most perfect one, the portrait of Mr. Rayfield's daughter, Edith.

We finally got the boxes and plates transferred to the adjacent building. A few days later, the bulldozer came and demolished the old barn. As days passed, I could not escape what I had seen and read regarding the printing plates, the pictures, and inscriptions. I felt compelled to find out more about Mr. Rayfield. I wanted to know who he was and where his firm had been located. I took a day off from my insurance business and began calling what seemed to be everyone in town, trying to find anyone who knew anything about Mr. Rayfield. I was referred from one person to another. It seemed that no one knew anything about him.

Just as I was about to give up, someone at the *Birmingham News* office suggested I call the Birmingham Historical Society. When a person there answered the phone, I asked if they had ever heard of the firm W. A. Rayfield & Co., Architects. They said they had. I asked them if it was a white or black firm. They replied, "Why do you want to know?" Upon my telling them of the discovery, they literally screamed with excitement, stating that they had been searching for twenty years trying to find virtually anything pertaining to Mr. Rayfield's life and work and could not find anything other than a few churches whose cornerstones bore his name.

Dr. Marjorie White of the Birmingham Historical Society asked permission to come to my home immediately and examine the find. She was ecstatic about the discovery and suggested contacting the *Birmingham News* and WBRC TV. Both sources quickly responded and covered the story. On November 6, 1993, with the Gulf War raging, the *Birmingham News* dedicated half the front page in color to the discovery. I was overwhelmed with the attention given the find and began to realize just how significant the cache really was.

Mrs. White told me about a booklet in the Birmingham Public Library titled *Wallace A. Rayfield Pioneer Black Architect of Birmingham, Alabama* by Charles A. Brown. It was a small booklet of about eight pages, much like a church program, but it contained a lot of information about Rayfield. While reading it I learned that Rayfield had been an instructor at Tuskegee Institute, so I phoned Tuskegee University to see what they could tell me about him. The person with whom I spoke could not tell me much but referred me to Vinson McKenzie, Architectural Librarian at Auburn University, who was reportedly in the process of researching a number of early black architects, including Robert Taylor and Wallace Rayfield. Upon learning of the discovery, Mr. McKenzie was anxious to examine the artifacts, so we made an appointment to meet.

In the meantime someone suggested that I have the artifacts appraised. I was referred to the Birmingham Museum of Art who referred me to Paul Sternburg, a professional appraiser from Marietta, Georgia, who appraised antiques, art, and rare artifacts. Mr. Sternburg made an appointment to examine the artifacts and then issued an official letter of authenticity and appraisal. I was astonished at the historic and financial worth of the artifacts. I then took steps to have them secured in a bank vault where they would be protected.

Around this time I became good friends with Steven G. Lightsey Sr., who held a degree in biblical studies from William Carey College in Hattiesburg, Mississippi, and his wife Delora, who held a degree in education from The University of Alabama. They both recognized the importance of the discovery and began sharing with me their vision of a book and an exhibition. They were a constant source of encouragement as we brainstormed about future possibilities.

Also, around this time I began learning about printing the

plates. Mr. Sternburg had made chalk rubbings from some of the plates that revealed beautiful images. This gave me a burning desire to pursue the possibilities of printing the plates. I phoned a number of old print shops in the Birmingham area. I eventually made contact with the Fairfield Printing Company. I explained to the owner what I had discovered and asked him if the plates could be printed. He told me they could be printed and invited me to bring one to him and he would show me how to print it. I carried one of the most elaborate plates to him. He walked back to an old mop sink, picked up a wet brass bristle brush, and began scrubbing the plate. I almost had a coronary. I shouted, "What are you doing?" He assured me that he knew what he was doing and that the scrubbing would not damage the plate. I was afraid he was going to totally destroy the image. I did not realize he was just cleaning off the old surface corrosion. When he finished, he dried it off, rolled it with ink, placed it in a proof press, and pulled the roller. Off came a gorgeous, beautiful print. I could hardly believe it. The printing fever gripped me and I had to have one of those antique proof presses. With his help, I began searching and shopping. I eventually located and bought two presses. I was now in the printing business. With help from Steve and Delora Lightsey, my wife Dorothy and I began printing Mr. Rayfield's plates. The prints were magnificent!

Finally the time came to meet with Mr. McKenzie, the architectural librarian at Auburn University. Steve went with me and suggested that I tape-record the meeting since it had the potential of becoming a future documentary. Mr. McKenzie was ecstatic about the discovery and declared that, in his opinion, it was the greatest discovery of the century pertaining to architectural history. He was especially excited because he had been trying to research Mr. Rayfield and like many others had been running into dead ends. He had very little information on Mr. Rayfield other than the above-mentioned booklet by Charles Brown and another book published in 1911 titled *Beacon Lights of the Race* by G. P. Hamilton, a copy of which was in the Birmingham Public Library Archives. After visiting for about an hour, we decided to set up a series of additional meetings at my home.

In the meantime I had recruited my brother Jim, James H. Durough Jr., and his wife Evelyn, who also helped with the printing. We worked tirelessly for weeks, printing the plates. In the process we learned that if we released to the public the "pulls" directly from the plates, we had no copyright protection since they comprised "works of antiquity" that would be in the public domain. However, we also learned that if we photographed the pulls, we could copyright the photographs and no one could copy them without our permission. Jim and I began photographing the pulls from the plates. It was a time consuming and expensive process, but we succeeded. On November 17, 1994, we completed the task and registered the photographs with the Library of Congress.

Additional meetings with Mr. McKenzie followed. Because

we all were now feeling that this had the potential of becoming a documentary, we decided to videotape each session. We also decided to enter into a collaboration agreement for the purpose of producing a book on the life and works of Mr. Rayfield.

Mr. McKenzie was entrusted with a complete photo album of the prints for reference and research purposes. His primary duty was to direct the team toward avenues of research and then with the team's help, compile the manuscript. The duties of the remaining team included doing the research, filing the collected data, cataloging the plates and prints, and compiling a spreadsheet. Steve and I interviewed and tape-recorded Dr. A. G. Gaston of Birmingham, Alabama, and a number of other people who either knew or had knowledge of Mr. Rayfield. Steve, Jim, and I spent hundreds of hours going through microfilm and old newspapers at the Birmingham Public Library.

Utilizing the information gathered, the team set out on numerous research ventures, particularly verifying building locations and photographing those that still existed. Mr. McKenzie contributed research from his travels to Florida, Georgia, and Kentucky. Steve and Delora contributed research from their trips throughout Alabama, Mississippi, and Florida. Dorothy and I contributed research from our trips throughout Alabama, Mississippi, Louisiana, Texas, and Arkansas. Jim, a BellSouth retiree with excellent computer skills, compiled the research into an extensive spreadsheet and contributed research from his trips to Tennessee; Washington, DC; Maryland; Georgia; and throughout Alabama. Jim also made a tremendous contribution by discovering approximately 125 original Rayfield or Rayfield-related letters at the Library of Congress in Washington, DC and the Freedmen's Aid Society Archives in Atlanta, Georgia.

As *The Architectural Legacy of Wallace A. Rayfield* rolls off the press, we hope that it will make a significant contribution to black history, architectural history, church history, and early American history. Also, we hope the catalog of buildings will help states, counties, and cities across America identify and preserve the many Rayfield buildings that still stand.

Acknowledgments

The author wishes to express his appreciation to all who helped in the research and assembly of this work, and apologizes in advance if he has unintentionally omitted anyone. He is deeply grateful to everyone who helped.

Teddy Abebe, archivist and professor, Howard University, Washington, DC; Rev. Ed Adams, pastor of First Christian Church, Jacksonville, Florida; Joe Aldredge, president of Commercial Printing Co., Birmingham, Alabama; Pauline Anderson, Tabernacle Baptist Church, Selma, Alabama; Hon. Richard Arrington, former mayor, City of Birmingham; Joe Athey, Trinity United Methodist Church, Cumberland, Maryland.

Jim Baggett, archivist, Birmingham Public Library; Amber Baker, student, History Department, The University of Alabama, Tuscaloosa, for research and work on the introduction; Julia Baker, assistant registrar of Talladega College, Talladega, Alabama; Loni Beagle, secretary, St. Paul Episcopal Church, Batesville, Arkansas; Dr. Dan Bennett, dean of the College of Architecture, Design, and Construction, Auburn University; Andrea Bittas, architect and assistant director, City of Birmingham Department of Planning, Engineering, and Permits; Rev. Claude Black, pastor, Mt. Zion Baptist Church, San Antonio, Texas; Victor Blackledge, architect, City of Birmingham; Rev. Arnold Blackmon, pastor, Seventeenth Street Macedonia Baptist Church, Birmingham, Alabama; Alta Bowman, historian, First Christian Church, White Oak, Oklahoma; Dr. Alice M. Bowsher, architectural historian, Birmingham, Alabama; Anne Brawner, historian, Seguin, Texas; Rev. Cedric Britt, pastor, Mt. Gilead Baptist Church, Fort Worth, Texas; Mrs. Charles Allen Brown, Birmingham, Alabama; Karen B. Brown, pastor, Marlinton Methodist Church, Marlinton, West Virginia; Pat Burroughs, secretary, First Baptist Church, Heavener, Oklahoma; Bennie Burton, Birmingham, Alabama; Anita Bynum, secretary, First Baptist Church Waldron, Arkansas.

Rev. Jerry Calquett, pastor, Lineville Baptist Church, Lineville, Alabama; Rev. Herbert Cartwright, pastor, First Missionary Baptist Church, Decatur, Alabama; Bill Cather, Cather Printing, Birmingham, Alabama; Richard Cawthon, chief architectural historian, Department of Archives & History, Jackson, Mississippi; Roger Dale Clark, computer consultant, Bessemer, Alabama; Sarah O. Cleary, secretary, First Presbyterian Church, Kannapolis, North Carolina; Barbara Clotfelter, Birmingham Public Library, Birmingham, Alabama; Dr. Bernice Coar Cobb, professor, Miles College, Fairfield, Alabama; Dr. Niyi Coker Jr., director, African American Studies Program, University of Alabama at Birmingham; Rev. Calvin E. Collins, pastor, New Zion Baptist Church, Greenwood, Mississippi; Patsy Corniffe, secretary, Ebenezer Baptist Church, Wilmington, North Carolina; Rev. Solomon Crenshaw, pastor, Broad Street Baptist Church, Birmingham, Alabama; Rev. Ronnie Crocket, pastor, Mt. Olive Baptist Church, Orange, Texas; Milburn Crow, city clerk and historian, Mound Bayou, Mississippi; Vivian Curry, registrar, Talladega College, Talladega, Alabama.

Daisy B. Davis, historian, Sixth Avenue Beulah Baptist Church, Bessemer, Alabama; Rev. Richard Davis, pastor, Gaines Chapel AME Church, Birmingham, Alabama; Dr. Richard Dozier, dean, School of Architecture, Florida A&M University; Samuetta Drew, City of Birmingham Board of Education; Father Albert Drilsch, priest, St. Francis Xavier Catholic Church, Moundsville, West Virginia; Rev. James Dunn, pastor, Morning Star Baptist Church, Demopolis, Alabama; Sally Durr, Epworth Methodist Church, Chickasha, Oklahoma.

Edwena Logan Edwards, historian, Allen Temple AME Church, Bessemer, Alabama; Dr. Lorenzo Edwards, pastor, Mt. Mariah Baptist Church, Ocala, Florida; Rev. Wedzell Escott, pastor, Trinity CME Church, Pratt City, Alabama; Rev. Truitt F. Evans, pastor, First Baptist Church, Brighton, Alabama.

Dr. Wilson Fallin Jr., professor of history, University of Montevallo and president, Birmingham-Easonian Baptist Bible College; Dr. Erskine Faush, WATV Radio, Birmingham, Alabama; Mr. and Mrs. Robert Fennoy, Miles College alumni; Dr. Kari Fredrickson, professor and director, Summersell Center for the Study of the South, Department of History, The University of Alabama.

Dr. A. G. Gaston, chairman of the board, Citizens Federal Savings Bank, Birmingham, Alabama; Joseph Giattina Jr., president, Giattina, Fisher & Company, Architects, Birmingham, Alabama; Rev. James Gibson, pastor, Greater Temple Baptist Church, Birmingham, Alabama; William A. Gilchrist, architect, and director, City of Birmingham Department of Planning, Engineering, and Permits; Rev. Thomas Gilmore, pastor, First Baptist Church, Ensley, Alabama; Rev. Steve Ginn, pastor, Central Christian Church, Jacksonville, Florida; Ellison Graham, The University of Alabama Press, for tireless and diligent work on this book; Sherri Griffin, photographer, Birmingham, Alabama; Lawton Grimes Jr., photographer, the *Western Star,* Bessemer, Alabama.

Angela Fisher Hall, archivist, Birmingham Civil Rights Institute; Rev. J. A. Hall, pastor, St. Paul AME Church, Tuscaloosa, Alabama; Dr. Christopher Hamlin, pastor, Sixteenth Street Baptist Church, Birmingham, Alabama; Earnest A. Hardy, director of research, Birmingham Board of Education; Rev. H. B. Harris, pastor, Mt. Mariah Baptist Church, Middlesboro, Kentucky; Rev. Ralph C. Harris, pastor, First Baptist Church, Winter Haven, Florida; Alfredteen Harrison, professor, Delta State University, and director of Margaret Walker National Research Center, Jackson, Mississippi; Viki Harrison, executive secretary to Dr. A. G. Gaston, Birmingham, Alabama; Steven Hawk, CBS 42 TV, Birmingham, Alabama; James Head Sr., president, Heads Inc., Birmingham, Alabama; Mrs. R. T. Hite, historian, Marlinton Presbyterian Church, Marlinton, West Virginia; Rev. Clinton Hubbard, pastor, St. Paul AME Church, Birmingham, Alabama; Willie Hughs, Fairfield Printing Company, Fairfield, Alabama; George Hunter Jr., president, George Hunter Jr. Architect & Associates, Birmingham, Alabama; Myra Hutchinson, great-niece of Bessie Rayfield Sneed, New York, New York; Rev. Albert L. Hyche, pastor, Payne Chapel AME Church Birmingham, Alabama.

Mrs. Fred Irwin, Rocky Springs Presbyterian Church, Laurens, South Carolina.

Dr. Carla Jackson, professor of architecture, Tuskegee University; Cleo Munson Jackson, historian, Second Baptist Church, Waco, Texas; Mattie Jackson, archivist and librarian, Miles College; Rosa Jackson, secretary, Roanoke Baptist Church, Hot Springs, Arkansas; Catherine Jelle, secretary, First Baptist Church, Covington, Kentucky; Clarance Johnson, Deacon, Macedonia Baptist Church, Altus, Oklahoma; Jennifer Johnson, historian, Avenue L Baptist Church, Galveston, Texas; Rev. Nathan Johnson, pastor, Antioch Baptist Church, Houston, Texas; Susan Johnson, secretary, First Baptist Church, Alpine, Texas; Bill Jones, Birmingham Historical Society; Casper Jones, office manager, East Mount Olive Baptist Church, Beaumont, Texas; Rev. Gerald F. Jones, pastor, St. James Baptist Church, Birmingham, Alabama; Rev. W. C. Jones, pastor, Bailey's Tabernacle CME Church, Tuscaloosa, Alabama; Rev. LeeRoy Jordan, pastor, First Baptist Church North, Tulsa, Oklahoma.

Elizabeth Kambourian, secretary, Mt. Olive Baptist Church, Richmond, Virginia; Mable Kennedy, secretary, St. John's Missionary Baptist Church, Oklahoma City, Oklahoma; Pat Kines, Columbia Baptist Church, Dothan, Alabama; Shannon Kirk, secretary, First Baptist Church, Blue Springs, Missouri; George Knight, photographer, for picture of Mt. Pilgrim Baptist Church in Milton, Florida.

Rev. James E. Lee, pastor, St. Matthews First Baptist Church, Clearwater, Florida; Rev. James Lewis, pastor, 23rd Street Baptist Church, Birmingham, Alabama; Delora Lightsey, photographer, for picture of Mt. Zion Baptist Church, Pensacola, Florida; Sue Lightsey, photographer, for picture, Providence Baptist Church, Laurel, Mississippi; J. H. Little, chairman of deacons, Hunter's Chapel AME Zion Church, Tuscaloosa, Alabama; Father John Loving, rector, Emmanuel Episcopal Church, San Angelo,

Texas; Dr. Leon Lowry, pastor, Beulah Baptist Institutional Church, Tampa, Florida; Jaime Lyons, student in the History Department at The University of Alabama, Tuscaloosa, for research and work on the introduction.

Julia Maglothin, secretary, South Avondale Baptist Church, Birmingham, Alabama; Rev. Rose Mancey, pastor, Vestal United Methodist Church, Knoxville, Tennessee; Rev. R. L. McAdory, pastor, First Baptist Church South, Bessemer, Alabama; Rev. Carlington McGlothan, pastor, 45th Street Baptist Church, Birmingham, Alabama; the late Vinson McKenzie, architectural librarian, Auburn University; Rector Jim McLean, St. Paul Episcopal Church, Batesville, Arkansas; Barbara Meigs, First Baptist Church, Cleveland, Oklahoma; Rev. Max Miller Jr., pastor, Friendship Baptist Church, Birmingham, Alabama; Ray Minor, director of development, Miles College; Deloris Mitchell, great-niece of Bessie Rayfield Sneed, Birmingham, Alabama; Dr. Marion J. Moore, Birmingham Civil Rights Institute; Rev. George Murray, pastor, Shady Grove Baptist Church, Birmingham, Alabama.

Linda Nelson, program manager, Bessemer Main Street, Bessemer, Alabama; Raymond Neth, Chandler Baptist Church, Liberty, Missouri; Bob Newton, editor, the *Eagle Democrat,* Warren, Arkansas.

Lydia Outen, secretary, First Baptist Church, Concord, North Carolina; Kenneth Owens, architect and partner, Owens & Woods, Architects, Birmingham, Alabama.

Rev. J. R. Parnell, pastor, Mt. Hebron Baptist Church, Irondale, Alabama; Rev. L. G. Patience, rector, Grace Episcopal Church, Lake Providence, Louisiana; Theodore Patton, former president, Smithfield Community, Birmingham, Alabama; Rev. Matthew Payne II, pastor, Mt. Zion Baptist Church, Pensacola, Florida; Rev. Chriss Perry, pastor, McCombs Chapel AME Church, Pratt City, Alabama; Tonte Peters, College of Architecture, Design & Construction, Auburn University; Rufus Points, Birmingham Board of Education; Ken Pool, director, Archives and Historic Preservation, Jackson, Mississippi; Alberta Porter, retired teacher and former tenant of W. A. Rayfield, Birmingham, Alabama; Rev. John Porter, pastor, Sixth Avenue Baptist Church, Birmingham, Alabama.

Wylheme Ragland, pastor, King's Memorial United Methodist Church, Decatur, Alabama; Charles Raine, architect, David Jones Jr. & Associates Inc., Birmingham, Alabama; Essie Rayford, Zion Travelers Baptist Church, Monroe, Louisiana; Rev. Michael Reese, pastor, New Zion Baptist Church, Bessemer, Alabama; Fred Richardson, historian, Stone Street Baptist Church, Mobile, Alabama; Rev. Ron Richeson, pastor, Trinity Lutheran Church, Maysville, Kentucky; Nancy Ridley, Birmingham Board of Education; Charles Rogers, historian and chairman of deacons, First Missionary Baptist Church, Decatur, Alabama; Debora Rogers, Protective Life Insurance Co., Birmingham, Alabama; Rev. C. E. Rowe, pastor, Star of Bethel Baptist Church,

Hendersonville, North Carolina; Anne Ruisi, *Birmingham News;* Rev. J. A. Rump, pastor, St. James AME Church, Birmingham, Alabama.

Rev. Dorosco Scarber Sr., pastor, Twenty-Fifth Avenue Baptist Church, Birmingham, Alabama; Dr. John Schnorenburg, professor of art history, University of Alabama at Birmingham; James Seed, historian, First Church of Christ Scientist, Charleston, West Virginia; James E. Seed, First Church of Christ Scientist, Charleston, West Virginia; Dr. J. L. Simpson, pastor, Weeping Mary Baptist Church, Tuscaloosa, Alabama; Rev. Karnie Smith, pastor, St. John AME Church, Birmingham, Alabama; Nelson Smith, architect, Birmingham, Alabama; Dr. Virginia Whatley Smith, professor of African American studies, University of Alabama at Birmingham; Rev. Willie Smith, pastor, Old Sardis Baptist Church, Birmingham, Alabama; Rev. Anthony Spurgeon, associate pastor, Trinity AME Church, Spartanburg, South Carolina; Dr. Paul Sternberg, Atlanta, Georgia; Dr. Harmon Stockdale, pastor, Mt. Lebanon Baptist Church, Louisville, Kentucky; David Strawn, historian, First Baptist Church, College Station, Texas; Rev. David Summerville, pastor, Thirgood Memorial CME Church, Birmingham, Alabama; Kita Syden, First Christian Church, Henryetta, Oklahoma; Dr. K. Everette Sylvester, associate dean and head, Department of Architecture, Tuskegee University.

Rev. Richardson Tankerson, pastor, Bethel AME Church, San Antonio, Texas; Kippy Tate, architect, director, State of Alabama Building Commission, Montgomery; Franzine K. Taylor, head, reference section, Department of Archives and History, Montgomery, Alabama; Michele Tran, student, History Department, The University of Alabama, Tuscaloosa, for research and work on the introduction; Lauren G. Trimm, student in the History Department, The University of Alabama, Tuscaloosa, for research and work on the introduction; Rev. Frank Tyes, pastor, Lively Hope Baptist Church, Pratt City, Alabama.

Don Veasey, curator of photographs, Archives Department, Birmingham Public Library.

Logan Ward, Staunton, Virginia; Carolyn Washington, Metropolitan AME Zion Church, Birmingham, Alabama; Rev. Perry C. Washington, pastor, Waymon Chapel AME Church, Decatur, Alabama; Ruby Waugh, Historian, First Baptist Church, Highland Park, Little Rock, Arkansas; Tommy V. Weir, Alabama Public Television; Dr. Ellen Weiss, professor of architectural history, Tulane University; Rev. C. C. Welch, pastor, First Baptist Church, Brighton, Alabama; Katie Ruth Wesley, Birmingham, Alabama; Rev. Michael Wesley, pastor, Shiloh Baptist Church, Birmingham, Alabama; Rev. John White, pastor, Rocky Springs Presbyterian Church, Laurens, South Carolina; Dr. Marjorie White, Birmingham Historical Society; Dr. Marvin Whiting, archivist, Birmingham Public Library; Dr. Donnell D. Williams, pastor, Hunter's Chapel AME Zion Church, Tuscaloosa, Alabama; Fred Williams, O. K. French Cleaners, Birmingham, Alabama; Rev. J. L. Williams, pastor, True Light Baptist Church, Hattiesburg, Mississippi; Rev. Earnest Wilson, pastor, Harmony Street Baptist Church, Birmingham, Alabama; Father Edward Wilson, rector, St. Mark's Episcopal Church, Birmingham, Alabama; Dr. Alex Woodall, archivist, Birmingham Southern College.

Rev. Willie E. Young, pastor, Tabernacle Baptist Church, Jacksonville, Florida.

A Note on the Illustrations

Some of the images reproduced in this volume are taken from Wallace A. Rayfield's original printing plates, several of which became damaged before their discovery by Allen Durough. Because so little information remains about Rayfield and his architecture, the more legible pulls from the damaged plates have been included.

The Architectural Legacy of Wallace A. Rayfield

Introduction

Wallace Augustus Rayfield was born May 10, 1873, in Macon, Georgia, amid the turmoil of Reconstruction.[1] Despite the chaotic political, social, and economic conditions plaguing white and black southerners alike, Rayfield's early years were surprisingly stable and comfortable. He was the only child of Augustus and Mary Rayfield, both listed in the census of 1880 as "mulatto." Macon was a bustling city and seat of Bibb County, a predominantly rural county of roughly 28,000 residents in the 1880s, with African Americans constituting a slight majority. Regarded as middle Georgia's commercial hub, Macon also boasted an emerging manufacturing sector. Nevertheless, the majority of Bibb County's black residents remained tied to the land or employed as domestic workers.[2] Rayfield's father was employed as a railroad porter for the Pullman Car Company, and his mother worked as a seamstress. They also were property owners. The Rayfield family was relatively more prosperous than their neighbors in the mixed-race Washington Avenue neighborhood. The majority of their neighbors worked as servants, laborers, and washerwomen—the typical employment options available to African Americans only a few years removed from slavery. The one exception was their next-door neighbor, a white man named Sullivan, who was a cabinetmaker. The connection among race, opportunity, and mobility on Washington Avenue is glaringly apparent in the public record. The white children on the block attended school, whereas the African American children, including young Wallace, age eight, were listed as "at home."[3]

The relative prosperity of the Rayfield family can be attributed to Augustus Rayfield's occupation. At the height of the railroad industry, around 1869, portering emerged as one of the most influential job opportunities available to African Americans. Railroad porters quickly became recognized as a symbol of increased "social status" among the black community.[4] The average annual pay for a railroad porter in 1890 was five hundred dollars, almost double what a man could make sharecropping. The porters' duties were vast and included cleaning, cooking, shoe shining, and most importantly, serving the white passengers. Journalist Larry Tye has discovered that many successful African American professionals in the twentieth century boasted a porter father or grandfather, and that African American porters laid the foundation for later black advancement.[5]

Rayfield received his early education at Lewis Intermediate and High School. For seven years, Rayfield received instruction from Lucy G. Laney, a noted African American educator. The child of slaves, Laney was raised in Macon and eventually became a member of the first graduating class of Atlanta University. After receiving a second degree from South Carolina State College, Laney returned to Macon to open her own school. Her first school enrolled five students and was held in the lecture room at the Christ Presbyterian Church. With critical financial support from northern missionaries, Laney built a thriving institution whose graduates went on to attend Ivy League universities. Laney proved to be a great influence on Rayfield, who quickly became recognized for his artistic talent.[6]

Young Wallace's personal life took a radical turn in 1885 with the death of his mother. Most likely because Augustus Rayfield's job as a railroad porter made it nearly impossible to raise a child on his own, guardianship of Wallace passed to an aunt, Clara Raglan, of Washington, DC.[7] The nation's capital in the late nineteenth century was an exciting place for a young boy from the Deep South. Following the abolition of slavery, Washington, DC, became the center of the nation's black aristocracy, home to a light-skinned and affluent elite that distanced themselves from the darker-skinned middle-class population while both ignored the "inarticulate blacks." Washington was also home to Howard University. Chartered in 1867, Howard is identified by one historian as the "first University south of the Mason-Dixon Line to be expressly dedicated to biracial education."[8] Rayfield was among the privileged young African Americans who took advantage of the opportunities for advancement available in the metropolis. In Washington, Rayfield became acquainted with a young white artist, Dela L. Mussey, who tutored Rayfield on Saturdays in her home. Dela's father was the attorney R. Delavan Mussey. Through the Mussey family Rayfield secured an apprenticeship with the prestigious A. B. Mullett and Company architectural firm, where Mussey served as a corporate attorney.

Alfred B. Mullett, an English immigrant, was well known for his French-style municipal buildings. Before his resignation in 1874, Mullett produced well-designed government buildings collectively worth over $50 million. The most famous of his many structures is the U.S. Treasury Department building. A hands-on architect, Mullett oversaw every detail of his plans, a characteristic that Rayfield appears to have acquired. Mullett's early work resembles a Renaissance Revival style or, in contrast, a simple classical mode. He also produced buildings in the Roman Doric design, characterized by grand stairs, giant pilasters, and wide overhangs. Rayfield remained at A. B. Mullett for two years, and his time there seems to have influenced his own architectural designs, which utilize characteristics of many architectural genres.[9]

While in Washington, Rayfield attended Howard University and graduated with a certificate from the Preparatory Department in 1896.[10] At age twenty-three, Rayfield enrolled in the Department of Architecture at Pratt Polytechnic Institute in Brooklyn, New York. Admissions requirements were exacting. Successful applicants were required to pass examinations in freehand drawing from ornament, simple casts, and objects; arithmetic, including fractions, percentages, proportion, square root, and mensuration; and in English grammar and composition. The architecture course of study at Pratt consisted of architectural drafting and rendering, freehand drawing, sketching, watercolor, mathematics, the history of architecture, and architectural design. Rayfield studied at Pratt for two years and received his certificate of graduation in 1899.[11] Following his graduation from Pratt, Rayfield enrolled in the Department of Architecture at Columbia University, and received the degree of Bachelor of Architecture.[12] According to the *Birmingham Age Herald,* Rayfield "topped off his training with a year's course of special work with the famous London (England) Polytechnic Institute."[13]

While still a student at Columbia University, Rayfield became acquainted with African American educator Booker T. Washington, who was visiting the campus. Washington offered Rayfield a teaching position at the Tuskegee Normal and Industrial Institute in Alabama following his graduation. In late 1899, Rayfield returned to the South, now a university-trained architect, to become an instructor of mechanical and architectural drawing at the center for industrial education, Tuskegee Institute.

The efforts of a former slave, Lewis Adams, to secure a school for African Americans in the Black Belt region of Alabama came to fruition 1881 with the founding of Tuskegee Normal and Industrial Institute.[14] Booker T. Washington, a prominent African American advocate, was chosen to lead the new school in the capacity of principle, administrator, and fund-raiser. Influenced by his years as a student and a teacher at Hampton Institute, Washington had a vision for Tuskegee Institute that centered on equipping students with the vocational skills necessary to better themselves and the community. At the institute, academic courses were designed to emphasize an industrial education. Students at Tuskegee were taught practical subjects such as dressmaking, masonry, agriculture, and carpentry.[15] The pragmatic and industrial nature of Tuskegee and its leader were particularly apparent in the early years of the institute's founding. Students applied classroom instructions on masonry to the greater community by constructing bricks needed for new buildings on campus. In doing so, the individuals learned an occupational trade and simultaneously earned income to finance their education.[16] The mission of an adult education appealed to many philanthropists, such as millionaire Andrew Carnegie, who made significant financial contributions to the school.[17]

The architectural program at Tuskegee was introduced in

1892. The program's objectives included the study of materials and their strengths, designing, architectural history, and freehand drawing. The program also stressed the value of labor and the importance of a strong work ethic.

During Wallace A. Rayfield's tenure as an instructor at Tuskegee Institute, the industrial drawing department underwent profound physical and curricular changes. Prior to his arrival, the classroom facilities of the department were rudimentary at best. The thirty-five students enrolled in the department were crammed inside a dim eight-by-twelve-foot room, which held several drawing tables constructed by nailing wooden boards to carpenter's saw benches. Under Rayfield's leadership, the department expanded to accommodate 320 students in 1901. In addition, the physical facilities of the Division of Architectural and Mechanical Drawing enlarged to encompass forty-seven drawing tables spread between two adjoining rooms illuminated by an abundance of natural light.[18]

Other programs within Tuskegee Institute benefited from the improvement of the industrial drawing department. In accordance with the practical nature of the institute, the architectural students sought to employ their industrial education in practical and useful ways. Students used blueprints as a tool to create items needed by other school programs, such as washstands, tables, and wagons. In addition, the division contributed to the growth of Tuskegee because it was responsible for developing the physical layout of the school.[19]

Rayfield also appears to have had a strong influence on the curriculum. By 1901, the curriculum had shifted to place more weight on drawing, construction, and design. Students were required to spend much of their time in the drawing room and attending lectures on a variety of subjects, such as lighting, heating, and plumbing.[20]

Motivated by a sense of professional pride and possibly the desire to leave behind a legacy, Rayfield sought to systematize teaching materials for the students in his department. In doing so, Rayfield developed an "Industrial Drawing Book" to bring a degree of validity or professionalism to the school. Rayfield intended for the "Industrial Drawing Book" to form the foundation of his courses through its role as a sort of textbook. The book included twenty-four illustrations and provided an overview of the elements of industrial drawing including the use of instruments and exercises to help with the projection method.[21]

When the manual was completed, Rayfield turned to his employer with the hope that his work would be printed by Tuskegee Institute. Through the mutual relationship, the school would have received monetary benefits, and Rayfield would have retained ownership rights to the work. The issue of publishing the manual played out in a series of letters among Rayfield, Booker T. Washington, and Robert R. Taylor, the then-director of industries for the school.

Judging by the available correspondence, Washington failed

to respond to Rayfield's request in what Rayfield considered a timely manner; Rayfield noted in one letter that he had been awaiting a decision for eight months.[22] Other issues related to the book furthered Rayfield's frustration. For one, Rayfield felt that Tuskegee Institute was charging too much for the simple handling of his book. Instead of the recommended 10 percent fee, the school wanted 20 percent. The financial conflicts combined with delays in printing the "Industrial Drawing Book" proved to be too much for Rayfield, and he offered his resignation from the position of instructor at Tuskegee Institute.[23] However, with Taylor serving as an intermediary, Rayfield was persuaded to withdraw his resignation, and the manual was ultimately published in 1904.

Over the years, there has been little mention of Rayfield's "Industrial Drawing Book." To the author's best knowledge, no one has recently been able to locate an original copy of it. However, the cover page of the book, the twenty-four main plates, and additional plates illustrating various drawing techniques are included in The Rayfield Collection of printing plates.

Rayfield was proficient at printing and was probably instrumental in helping Tuskegee acquire a new printing press in 1904. The volume of printing within the institution and Rayfield's exacting standards for high-quality work made the purchase of a new printing press imperative. The press, called "the Optimus," allowed the school to do even better, higher-quality work.[24]

In addition to crafting his book for use in the classroom, Wallace Rayfield put his architectural skills and experience to good use by teaching private lessons during the summer. This employment probably helped supplement his meager salary as a teacher. During the summer of 1907, Rayfield advertised in newspapers his services in areas including "free-hand drawing (pencil), pen and ink, water colors, charcoal work and mechanical work." Classes were offered for a variety of ages from children and older students to adults. The costs ranged from two dollars to three dollars for the entire eight weeks, half of which was to be paid in advance.[25]

The hassle surrounding the "Industrial Drawing Book" contributed to Rayfield's growing disenchantment with his arrangements at Tuskegee. In 1900, Rayfield and other members of the faculty drafted a petition to Booker T. Washington protesting the stringent mealtime policy that often resulted in a student happily denying entrance into the dining hall to any faculty member who was even a minute late.[26] Later, Washington reprimanded the instructor for failing to abide by school rules when he was caught smoking by the side of the road near the school.[27] Also, Rayfield constantly felt underpaid and restricted intellectually. In 1904, he complained to Taylor that "the great demand on my position calls for more research work and study, [and] this necessitates books, magazines, study and travel"; the architect's meager yearly salary of $540 (only slightly more than what his father earned as a porter in the 1880s) was insufficient.[28] Subsequently, Rayfield approached Taylor for a raise. Taylor, endeavoring to keep Rayfield at Tuskegee Institute, approved an increase of five dollars a month in the teacher's pay. In his recommendation of the salary increase to Booker T. Washington, Taylor explained that "Mr. Rayfield is a painstaking man; he goes to some expense for the purchase of books bearing on his line. If his salary was increased $5.00 per month I do not think it would be exorbitant at all."[29]

Amid a growing dissatisfaction with his life at Tuskegee, Rayfield enjoyed some personal happiness. In 1901 he married Jennie M. Hutchins. A native of Clarksville, Tennessee, Ms. Hutchins was a graduate of the industrial department of Tuskegee. Rayfield also took a professional risk and ventured into private practice, opening his first official architectural office in 1907. His main office was in the Court Square at Tuskegee with branch offices in Birmingham, Montgomery, and Mobile, Alabama, as well as in Atlanta, Macon, Savannah, and Augusta, Georgia.

Exercising his entrepreneurial spirit, Rayfield began advertising immediately. He advertised plans for cottages, schools, and churches. He also advertised a connection with W. T. Adams, a well-known contractor.

Within a brief period, Rayfield was advertising his successful contracts with schools in Florida, South Carolina, and Birmingham.[30]

Despite Taylor's best efforts and perhaps because of his success in private practice, Rayfield resigned his position at Tuskegee on September 23, 1907. Booker T. Washington, after his initial refusal to do so, later accepted the resignation and even wrote Rayfield a personal letter of recommendation.[31] Rayfield moved to Birmingham the following year.[32]

The center of the South's coal and iron production, Birmingham was home to a burgeoning black industrial working class and a growing black middle class. Birmingham's black middle class was greatly influenced by Washington's philosophy of self-help and accommodation. A few of the city's prominent race leaders had attended the Tuskegee Institute, while many others were active in Washington's National Negro Business League. Still other graduates of Hampton and Tuskegee played prominent roles in the various "negro welfare associations." Birmingham's black leadership was decidedly conservative, with philosophies that must have felt familiar to Rayfield from his Tuskegee days.[33]

Rayfield's first Birmingham office was at 1717-1/2 3rd Avenue in the Mason Building.[34] At that time, the Mason Building was home to many other African American businesses, including the Birmingham *Reporter* and the Birmingham *Messenger* newspapers. The Mutual Drug Store Association and Mutual Aid also claimed offices in the building. Rayfield moved his office location several times during his life.[35] Other locations include 310 18th Street, where the architectural firm resided in room 101 of the Alabama Penny Savings Bank Building. The building was later renamed the Pythian Temple. Similar

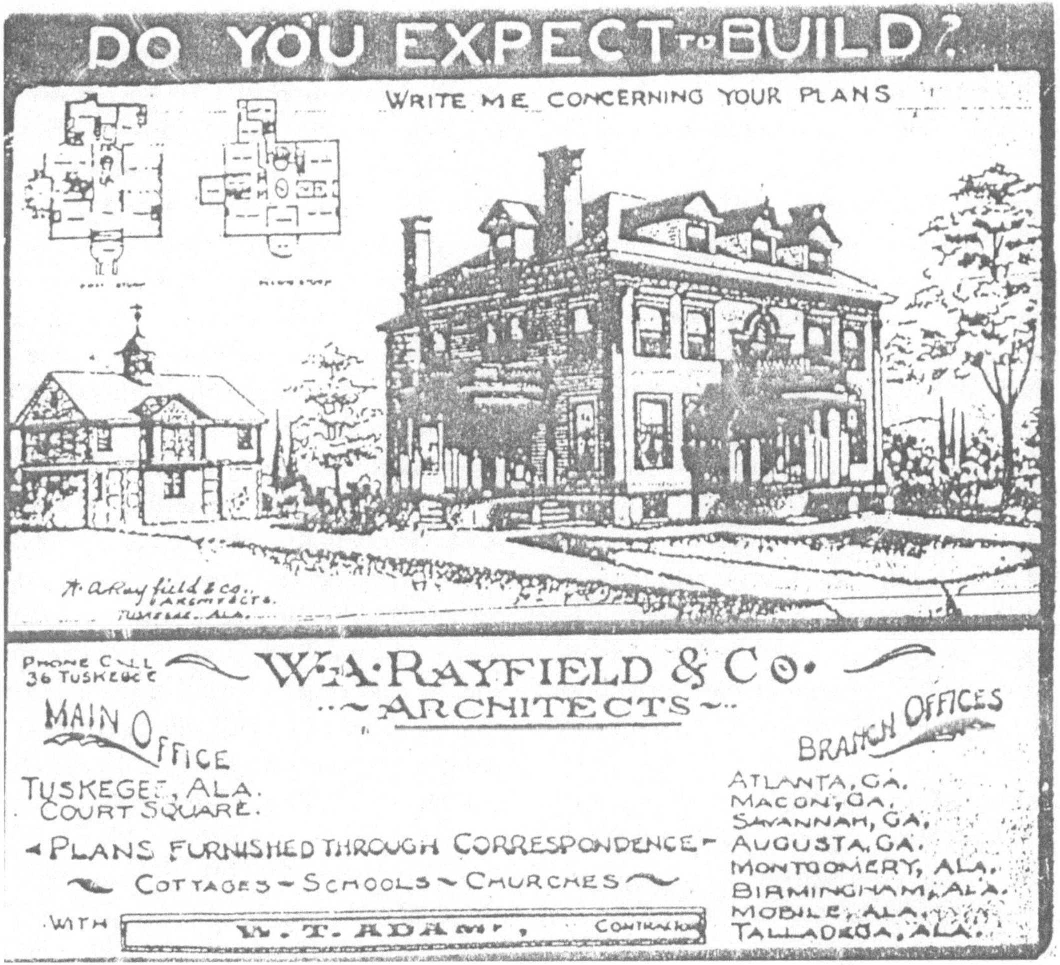
DO YOU EXPECT TO BUILD?
WRITE ME CONCERNING YOUR PLANS
PHONE CALL 36 TUSKEGEE
W. A. RAYFIELD & CO.
ARCHITECTS
MAIN OFFICE
TUSKEGEE, ALA.
COURT SQUARE.
PLANS FURNISHED THROUGH CORRESPONDENCE
COTTAGES – SCHOOLS – CHURCHES
BRANCH OFFICES
ATLANTA, GA.
MACON, GA.
SAVANNAH, GA.
AUGUSTA, GA.
MONTGOMERY, ALA.
BIRMINGHAM, ALA.
MOBILE, ALA.
TALLADEGA, ALA.
WITH
CONTRACTOR

to the first location of the company, the building housed many of the city's black professionals, doctors, dentists, and lawyers.[36] In the mid-1920s, Rayfield relocated his practice to his home, where he appears to have spent the remaining years of his professional life.[37]

His first known residence in the city, according to the 1909 Birmingham City Directory, was 109 Corrilla Street. Corrilla Street was also home to many other African Americans at that time. Later that same year, he relocated to a residence at 105 First Avenue in the Titusville Community. According to historian Phillip W. Holland, Rayfield's home was considered one of ten historical African American homes in Birmingham as it was "designed, financed, and built exclusively by local blacks." The upper level featured a naturally lighted drawing room with over a dozen windows that were accented by a large stained glass window. In this room Mr. Rayfield performed much of his work, producing many of his blueprints and drawings in the comfort of his home.[38] The community surrounding his home on 105 First Avenue was similar to that of his previous address. His neighbors were clergymen, railroad workers, and a variety of laborers.[39]

The Smithfield Neighborhood, near Rayfield's home in Titusville, was a district within Birmingham that was largely dominated by African Americans, particularly those belonging to the middle class.[40] Many of the residential and business buildings were built according to the designs of Wallace A. Rayfield. Prominent residents held occupations as doctors, lawyers, or church ministers. The occupations of these professionals differed markedly from those of the greater African American population in Birmingham during the first half of the twentieth century. In 1940, the U.S. Bureau of the Census recorded Birmingham's total population at 267,583, of which 41 percent were African American. Within that cohort, only 484 nonwhites held professional or semiprofessional positions.[41]

Rayfield's family became firmly ensconced within Birmingham's emerging black middle class. Jennie Hutchins Rayfield joined the famous Twentieth Century Club, serving as its president from time to time. She was a member of Saint Mark's Episcopal Church and was held in high regard in the community. After a long illness she died in 1929 and was buried in the family plot at Grace Hill Cemetery.[42]

Rayfield's only child was Edith Rayfield, who successfully completed college and taught school at Council Elementary in Ensley, Alabama.[43] She was married twice, first to Walter Blyth, a fellow teacher at Council Elementary, then later to Edward Johnson, a firefighter from the North. Edith had no children and died in 1989, leaving her residence to her niece, Julia Sargent Mitchell. Edith Josephine Rayfield Johnson's last residence was 5780 Jefferson Street, Philadelphia.

Rayfield remarried in 1932, to Bessie Rogers, a domestic worker employed by two Birmingham physicians. The couple lived at Rogers's home at 328 Iota Avenue in Birmingham. Bessie Rogers

Rayfield Sneed lived to be over one hundred years old and died in August 1989.[44]

As a member of the black middle class, and as the region's only black architect, Rayfield had a profound impact on the region's built environment. He designed homes for Birmingham's black leaders, churches for the community's congregations, and schools for its children. Arthur McKinnon Brown, one of the first black physicians in the city of Birmingham and a resident of Smithfield, commissioned Rayfield to design his home in the neighborhood. The resulting design, a two-story house consisting of nine separate rooms, exists in present-day Birmingham at 319 Fourth Terrace North. The doctor's home has been remodeled into the present-day A. M. Brown Community Center for Arts and Crafts. Rayfield's influence in the area can also be seen in the gabled cottage-style home of neighbors Arthur H. Parker and E. A. Brown, attorney and Arthur Brown's brother.[45]

Often working in conjunction with Rayfield was Thomas C. Windham, a noted African American building contractor who, together with his brother, operated a construction firm in Birmingham that was in business for approximately seventy-five years.[46] Windham was commissioned to construct the Trinity Baptist Church in the Smithfield Neighborhood as well as the Sixteenth Street Baptist Church, a Rayfield design, in Birmingham.[47]

Rayfield's growing reputation was instrumental in securing

significant endorsements and supervisory positions with national organizations. Rayfield served as the Connectional Architect for the AME Zion Church, essentially the official architect for the church throughout the nation and Africa. He was appointed the General Supervising Architect of the Freedmen's Aid Society. Founded in 1866 as an agency of the Methodist Episcopal Church, the society dedicated itself to establishing schools and churches for southern blacks. Rayfield also received an endorsement from the National Baptist Churches and Schools, a type of referral to independent Baptist congregations.

For the duration of Rayfield's professional life, Birmingham's (and the South's) cadre of architects remained small; African American architects were even more rare. In 1920, there were only forty-two individuals, all of whom were male, employed as architects in Birmingham, Alabama.[48] Ten years later, the number in the profession increased slightly to fifty-seven and included a sole female.[49] During that time, the African American population in Birmingham experienced a sharp increase from 70,230 in 1902 to a little over 99,000 the following decade. Yet as late as 1940, Rayfield remained the city's only African American architect.

The Great Depression hit Birmingham particularly hard. The rate of unemployment in Birmingham was double the national average, with half of all households devoid of any income. Within such dire economic circumstances, the services of an architect were considered a luxury, and Rayfield's business fell off

considerably. Plagued by declining economic fortunes, Rayfield suffered a paralytic stroke and died on February 28, 1941. His funeral service was conducted at the Immaculate Conception Catholic Church on Birmingham's south side. He was buried in the Greenwood/Woodlawn Cemetery "in section 5 at the juncture of 103, 102, 72, and 73."[50]

Notes

The author is grateful for the research assistance provided by University of Alabama history undergraduate students Amber Baker, Amber Cheung, Jaime Lyons, Michele Tran, and Lauren G. Trimm.

1. Discrepancies regarding Rayfield's birth date abound in primary

and secondary sources, ranging from 1872 to 1874. Rayfield himself listed his birth date as May 10, 1873, upon registering for the draft. See Selective Service Registration, Jefferson County, Alabama, Roll 150359, Draft Board.

2. Population data from the University of Virginia Library's Historical Census browser, available at http://fisher.lib.va.edu.

3. U.S. Bureau of the Census, 1880; Macon, Bibb County, Georgia; Roll T9-135; Family History Film 1254135; Page 221.3000; Enumeration District 15; Image 0083; Directory of the City of Macon (Georgia), 1880 (Macon, GA: J. W. Burke, 1880), 194. For the Rayfields' property ownership, see General Index to Real Estate Conveyances, Grantees Book O-P-Q-R-S, 1823–1919, p. 19, Bibb County, Georgia, Superior Court; General Index to Real Estate Conveyances, Grantors Book, Index to Deeds and Mortgages, Book N-O-P-Q-R, 1823–1919, p. 13, Bibb County, Georgia, Superior Court.

4. Jack Santino, *Miles of Smiles, Years of Struggle: Stories of Black Pullman Porters* (Urbana: University of Illinois Press, 1989).

5. Larry Tye, *Rising from the Rails: Pullman Porters and the Making of the Black Middle Class* (New York: Henry Holt, 2004).

6. For information on Lucy G. Laney see Jessie Carney Smith and Shirelle Phelps, eds., *Notable Black American Women* (Detroit: Gale, 2003), 650–62; *Atlanta Journal Constitution,* February 11, 1989, 1-C; G. P. Hamilton, *Beacon Lights of the Race* (Memphis: E. M. Clark and Brother, 1911), 452.

7. Petition for Guardianship, February 23, 1889, in Docket and General Index to Proceedings of Estates, Book R, 182301964, p. 189, Court of Ordinary, Bibb County, Georgia; Charles A. Brown, *W. A. Rayfield: Pioneer Black Architect of Birmingham, ALA* (Birmingham, AL: Gray Printing, 1972), 2. Clara Raglan appears in the 1870 census for Macon. The enumerator listed her as twelve years old, which would make her twenty-seven years old when she became Wallace Rayfield's guardian. The Washington, DC, city directory lists her employment as "seamstress." See Washington, D.C. City Directory, 1890, accessed through AncestryLibrary.com.

8. Constance McLaughlin Green, *The Secret City: A History of Race Relations in the Nation's Capital* (Princeton, NJ: Princeton University Press, 1967), 89, 120, 121; Elizabeth Clark-Lewis, *First Freed: Washington D.C. in the Emancipation Era* (Washington, DC: Howard University Press, 2002), 129.

9. Lawrence Wodehouse, "Alfred B. Mullett and His French Style Government Buildings," *Journal of the Society of Architectural Historians* 31 (March 1972): 22–27; Hamilton, *Beacon Lights of the Race,* 453.

10. Howard University, Alumni Directory, partial, furnished by Howard University archivist to A. Durough.

11. Catalogue, Pratt Institute, 1897–98 (Brooklyn, NY: Pratt Institute, 1898), 53; Handwritten Graduation List, 1898, Pratt Institute Archives, Pratt Institute, Brooklyn, New York.

12. Hamilton, *Beacon Lights of the Race,* 453. Despite their best efforts, the author and associated researchers were not able to locate a primary source that confirms Rayfield's tenure at Columbia University; however, Booker T. Washington later attested to Rayfield's credentials in a letter of recommendation for him.

13. Birmingham *Age Herald,* Silver Jubilee Issue, June 18, 1913.

14. Louis R. Harlan, *Booker T. Washington: The Making of a Black Leader* (New York: Oxford University Press, 1972), 113–14.

15. Virginia Lantz Denton, *Booker T. Washington and the Adult*

Education Movement (New York: Oxford University Press, 1993), 84, 96, 108.

16. Harlan, *Booker T. Washington,* 144–45.

17. Ibid., 274.

18. Emmett J. Scott, "Training Head and Hand: Architectural and Mechanical Drawing at Tuskegee," *The Tuskegee Student,* April 20, 1901, 1, 4.

19. Scott, "Training Head and Hand," 1, 4.

20. Richard Dozier, "Tuskegee: Booker T. Washington's Contribution to the Education of Black Architects" (PhD diss., University of Michigan, 1990), 37–68.

21. *The Tuskegee Student,* October 15, 1904.

22. Wallace A. Rayfield to R. R. Taylor, April 26, 1904, Departmental File—Mechanical Industries, Container 597, Robert R. Taylor folder, Booker T. Washington Papers, Library of Congress, Washington, DC (hereafter cited as BTWP).

23. R. R. Taylor to Booker T. Washington, August 5, 1905, Departmental File—Mechanical Industries, Container 606, BTWP.

24. R. R. Taylor to Booker T. Washington, November, 11, 1904, Departmental File—Mechanical Industries, Container 598, Robert R. Taylor folder, BTWP.

25. *The Tuskegee Student,* May 4, 1907.

26. Louis R. Harlan and Raymond W. Smock, eds., *The Booker T. Washington Papers: Volume 5, 1899–1900* (Urbana: University of Illinois Press, 1977), 410–11.

27. Louis R. Harlan and Raymond W. Smock, eds., *The Booker T. Washington Papers: Volume 6, 1901–1902* (Urbana: University of Illinois Press, 1977), 102.

28. Wallace A. Rayfield to Robert R. Taylor, March 7, 1904, Departmental File—Mechanical Industries, Container 597, Robert R. Taylor Folder, BTWP.

29. R. R. Taylor to Booker T. Washington, September 16, 1904, Departmental File—Mechanical Industries, Container 598, Robert R. Taylor Folder, BTWP.

30. See *The Tuskegee Student,* July 6, 1907.

31. Brown, *W. A. Rayfield,* 2; Booker T. Washington to "Whom It May Concern," August 15, 1908, Reel/Folder 525, Freedmen's Aid Society Records, Robert W. Woodruff Library, Atlanta University Center, Atlanta, Georgia.

32. Hamilton, *Beacon Lights of the Race,* 456.

33. For Birmingham's black middle class see Brian Kelly, *Race, Class, and Power in the Alabama Coalfields, 1908–1921* (Urbana: University of Illinois Press, 2001), 81–107; and Lynne B. Feldman, *A Sense of Place: Birmingham's Black Middle Class Community, 1890–1930* (Tuscaloosa: The University of Alabama Press, 1999).

34. Birmingham City Directory, 1911, 746.

35. Birmingham City Directory, 1912, 1236 and Birmingham City Directory, 1913, 996.

36. Birmingham City Directory, 1913, p. 1104; also see Kelly, *Race, Class, and Power in the Alabama Coal Fields,* 100.

37. Birmingham City Directory, 1926.

38. Brown, *W. A. Rayfield,* 2.

39. U.S. Bureau of the Census, Characteristics of Population, 1910.

40. Beth L. Savage and Carol D. Shull, *African American Historic Places* (Washington, DC: Preservation Press, 1996), 91.

41. U.S. Bureau of the Census, Characteristics of Population, 1940.

42. Brown, *W. A. Rayfield,* 3.

43. Ibid.

44. Bessie Rayfield Sneed Obituary, *Birmingham News,* August 17, 1989.

45. Feldman, *Sense of Place,* 66.

46. Savage and Shull, *African American Historic Places,* 89.

47. Feldman, *Sense of Place,* 62.

48. U.S. Bureau of the Census, 1920 Census, Characteristics of the Population.

49. U.S. Bureau of the Census, 1930 Census, Characteristics of the Population.

50. Brown, *W. A. Rayfield,* 8; Katherine Kent Lambert, "Birmingham," *Chicago Defender,* March 15, 1941.

1 Rayfield as Residence Architect

When Rayfield went into private practice, he created a number of his own advertisements in order to make himself known to prospective clients. As one part of his advertising material, Rayfield produced the *Southern Bungalow Book,* which complements and expands upon his other residential advertisements. It contained plans with pictures of bungalows, descriptions, costs, and advertisements for furnishings. The following is a partial reconstruction of that book based on some of the material available in The Rayfield Collection of printing plates.Additionally, Rayfield offered landscaping advice as well as recommendations for groups of workers he considered to be skilled and hard working. With the help of these advertisements, Rayfield became fairly successful and well known, particularly in the Birmingham area. However, only a few specimens of his work as a residence architect remain.

CONTENTS

This Book Contains One Hundred (100) Plans and Pictures of

BUNGALOWS

1

The cost of each plan and estimate of materials.

2

Plan of the floor, giving size of rooms and porches.

3

The arrangement of doors, windows, stairs and entrances.

4

Quality of materials used in the construction.

5

Height of ceiling and shape of ceiling in rooms.

6

How heated and lighted.

7

Location of fireplaces, furnace room and attic rooms.

8

General specifications and bill of materials with each plan.

9

Shape of roof, covering of roof, plumbing, electric wiring and call bells. Beam ceiling, plate racks, panelling, coal chute.

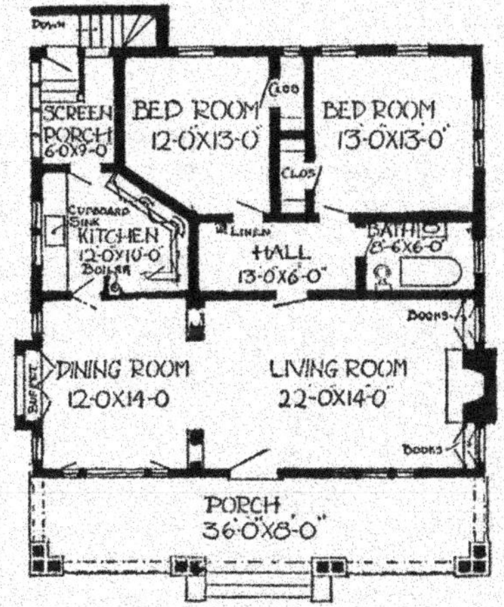

THE "JENNETTE"

The above building can be constructed

For $3,000

The plans and specifications complete $10.00 for above building

SPECIAL PLANS

We desire to co-operate with you in your individual ideas and will be glad to make sketches of your ideas free.

Price for Special Plans, 2 per cent of the cost of the Building.

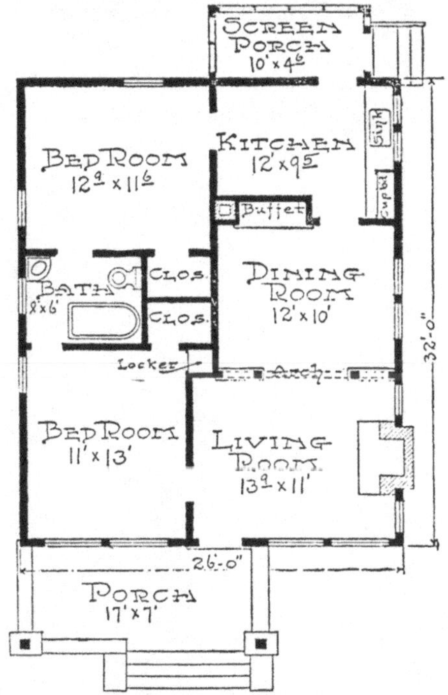

The MASON (U. G.) Bungalow

The simple straight lines have made this bungalow a pronounced favorite. Many unique decorative features are incorporated in this design. The small divided lights in the upper part of the windows have an air of delicacy that is balanced by bracketed projections. A wide open porch conforms to the simple lines employed throughout. The living room adjoins the dining room, separated by French doors.

Cost to Build, $3,000 to $4,000; Plans and Specifications, $20.00

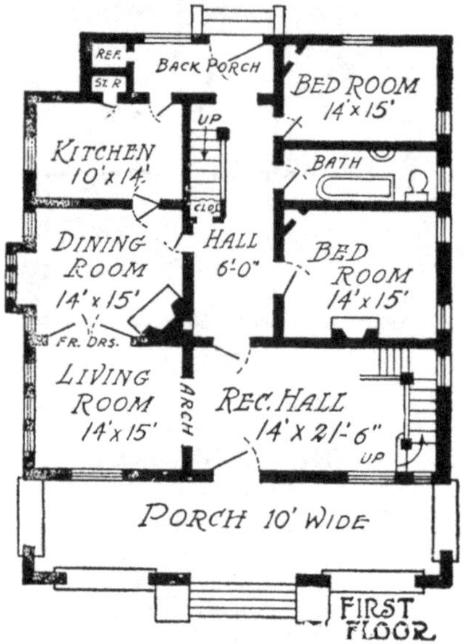

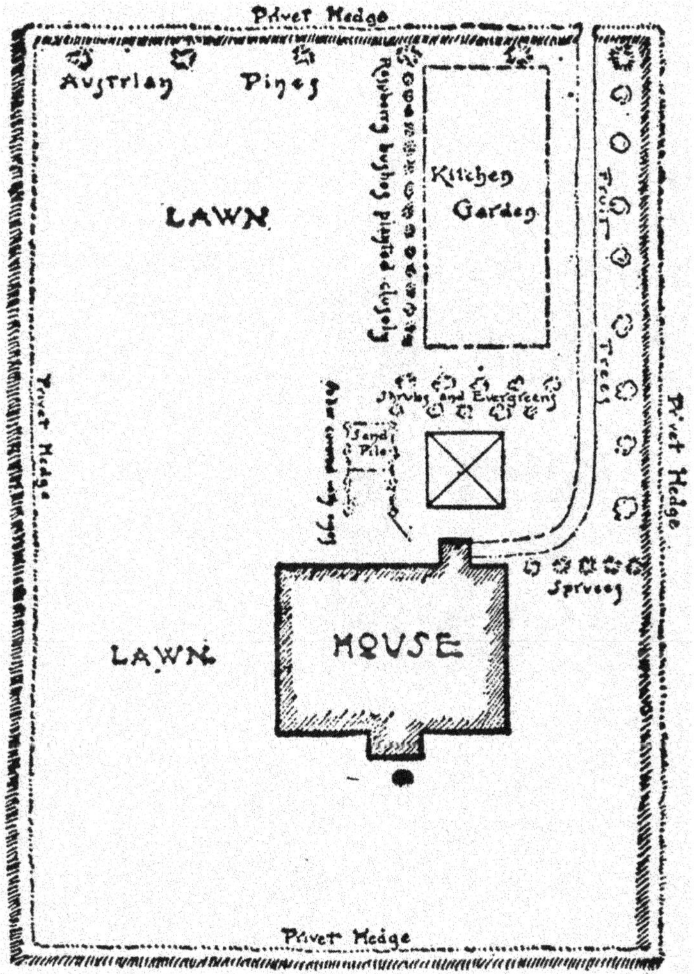
Privet Hedge
Austrian Pines
LAWN
Kitchen Garden
Fruit Trees
Shrubs and Evergreens
Sand Pile
HOUSE
Spruces
LAWN
Privet Hedge
Privet Hedge
Privet Hedge

The
COLORED
MECHANICS
OF
BIRMINGHAM, ALA.
COMPILED BY
W. A. RAYFIELD & CO.
ARCHITECTS
BIRMINGHAM, ALA.
DELIVERED FREE

The home of Richard A. Blount, the Grand Chancellor of the Knights of Pythias, was constructed in 1914 for $5,000 at the address of 322 6th Avenue North, Birmingham, Alabama. It has since been demolished. Photo courtesy of the Jefferson County Historical Society, "Historic Sites of Jefferson County Alabama," by Carolyn Green Satterfield, PhD.

The home of Arthur McKinnon Brown, a prominent doctor and the founder of the Children's Home Hospital in Birmingham, was constructed in 1918 at the address of 319 4th Terrace North, Birmingham, Alabama. Photo by Ellison Graham.

The home of Edward A. Brown, professional attorney and Grand Attorney for the Knights of Pythias, was constructed in 1908 at the address of 526 5th Street North, Birmingham, Alabama.

The home of Bishop R. T. Brown, a president of Miles College, was constructed circa 1926 at the address of 470 1st Street North, Birmingham, Alabama. Photo by Ellison Graham.

The home of Madam Clisby, a successful businesswoman, was built in 1919 at the address of 707 14th Street South, Birmingham, Alabama, at a cost of $15,000.

The home of Albert G. Dobbins, a teacher and principal of Lincoln Middle School, was constructed in 1926 at the address of 464 1st Street North, Birmingham, Alabama.

The home of Charles D. Ellison, a white salesman, was constructed in 1913 at the address of 7014 1st Street North, Birmingham, Alabama, for $3,000.

The home of W. H. Hudson was built in 1915 at the address of 329 A Street, Anniston, Alabama, for $4,000.

The home of Arthur H. Parker, who organized the first high school for blacks in Birmingham, was constructed in 1908 at the address of 522 5th Street North, Birmingham, Alabama, next door to E. A. Brown's home (previously pictured).

The Smith-Gaston home was constructed at the address of 120 57th Street, Fairfield, Alabama.

The home of Dr. Fred H. Strawbridge was constructed at 616 27th Street South, Birmingham, Alabama. It was demolished in the year 2000.

2 Rayfield as Church Architect

Church architecture was Rayfield's main area of interest. He created numerous advertisements for churches, as he did with his residential architecture. Rayfield also produced a number of books related to this field, including *Book of Designs: Churches* and his books of plans for various denominations such as *Plans for Baptist Churches, Plans for M.E. Churches,* and *Designs for Lutheran Churches.*

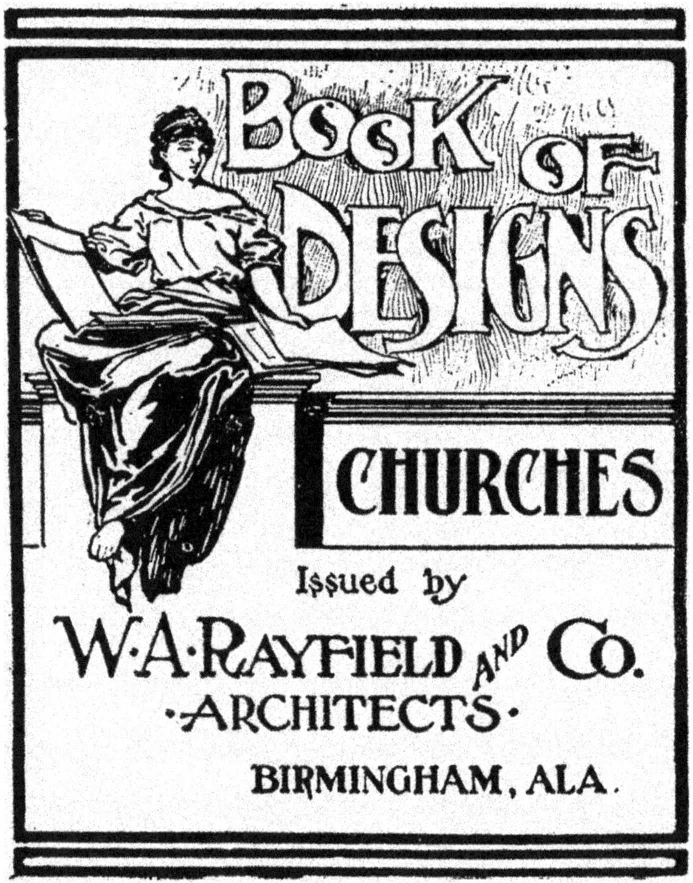
Book of Designs
Churches
Issued by
W·A·Rayfield and Co.
·Architects·
Birmingham, Ala.

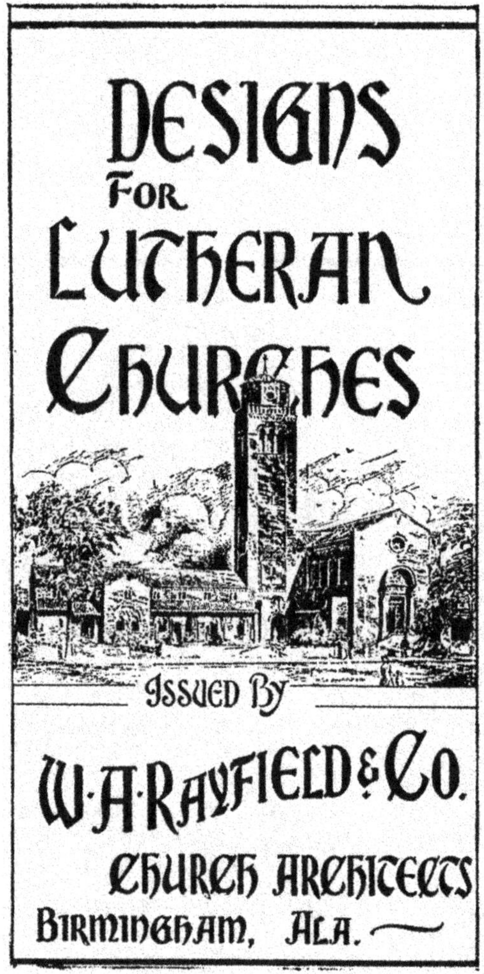
Designs for Lutheran Churches
Issued By
W·A·Rayfield & Co.
Church Architects
Birmingham, Ala.

In his books of plans, Rayfield incorporated a number of advertisements regarding church furnishings and fixtures along with his elevation drawings and floor plans. His church advertisements were circulated in various newspapers, magazines, books, and denominational publications. He made a great effort in advertising and designing churches based on a specific denomination and included many sample floor plans in his advertisements. Following is a catalog of known Rayfield churches around the United States.

PLAN AND PERSPECTIVE OF SMALL EPISCOPAL CHURCH.
Seating capacity, 160 to 200. Cost in brick, about $4,000.

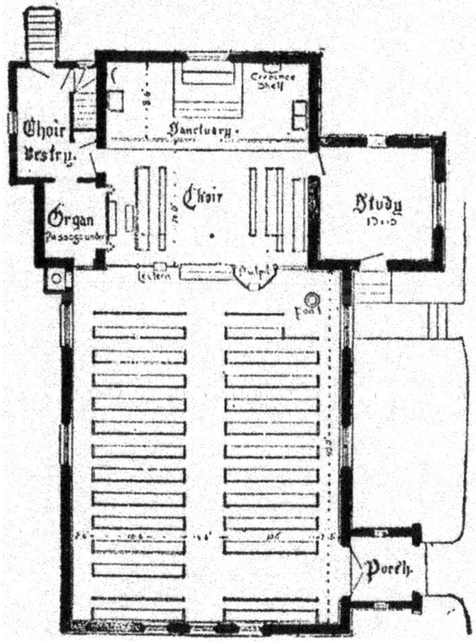

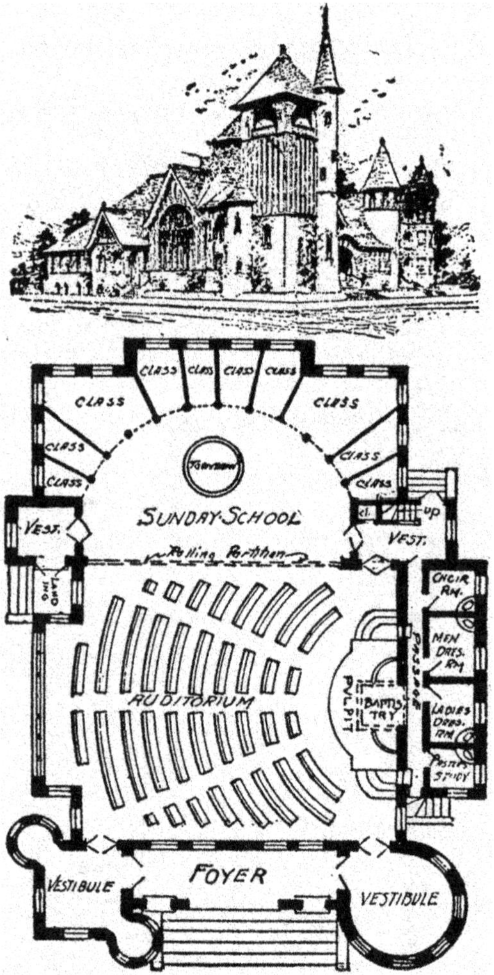
CLASS
CLASS
CLASS
CLASS
CLASS
CLASS
CLASS
CLASS
CLASS
CLASS
SUNDAY-SCHOOL
VEST.
VEST.
up
Rolling Partition
AUDITORIUM
PULPIT
BAPTIS-TRY
CHOIR RM.
MEN DRES. RM
LADIES DRES. RM
PASTOR'S STUDY
FOYER
VESTIBULE
VESTIBULE

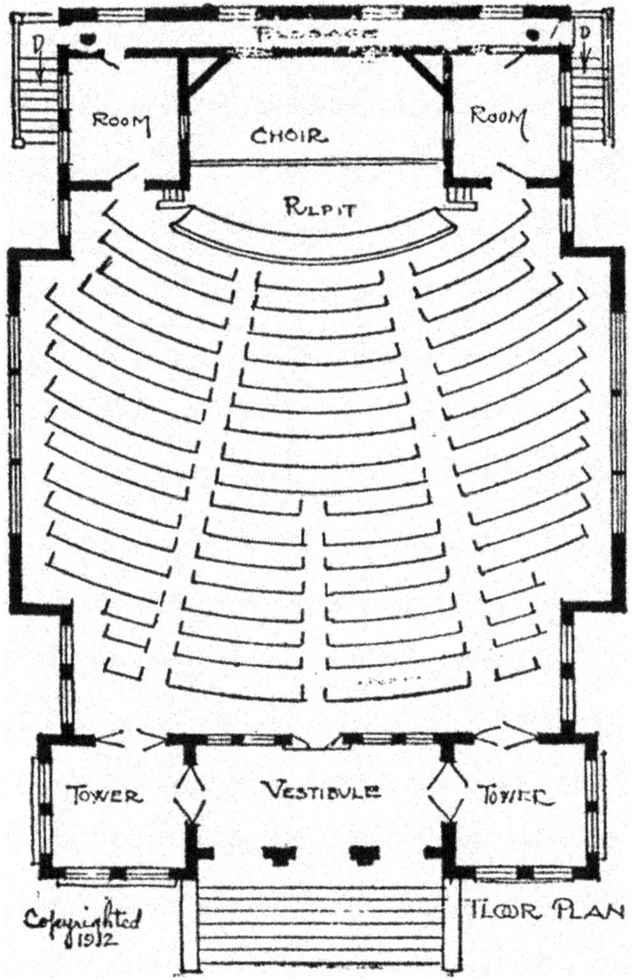
ROOM
CHOIR
ROOM
PULPIT
TOWER
VESTIBULE
TOWER
Copyrighted 1912
FLOOR PLAN

Allen Temple AME Church was constructed circa 1911 for $5,000 in Bessemer, Alabama. The church has since been rebuilt. Courtesy of Allen Temple AME Church.

Although the Allen Temple AME church has been rebuilt, the cornerstone from the original building, with W. A. Rayfield named architect, has been preserved and mounted on the new building. Cornerstones such as this one often appear on Rayfield's churches.

Bailey's Tabernacle CMEC Church was constructed in 1914 at the address of 23rd Avenue and 12th Street, Tuscaloosa, Alabama, for $12,000.

Beulah Baptist Church was constructed in 1917 at 2701 6th Avenue North, Bessemer, Alabama, for $8,000. Courtesy of the *Western Star,* Bessemer, Alabama.

Broad Street Baptist Church was constructed circa 1914 at the address of 110 North Broad Street, Birmingham, Alabama, at a cost of $7,000.

Day Street Missionary Baptist Church was built circa 1910 at the address of 861 Day Street, Montgomery, Alabama. Photo by Ellison Graham.

First Baptist Church was constructed in 1916 at the address of 203 North 4th Street, Alpine, Texas.

First Baptist Church was constructed in 1917 at the corner of West Avenue C and Second Street, Heavener, Oklahoma. It has since been demolished.

First ME Church South, now Marlinton United Methodist Church, was constructed circa 1922 at the address of 806 6th Avenue, Marlinton, West Virginia, costing $60,000. Courtesy of Marlinton United Methodist.

First Missionary Baptist Church was constructed in 1921 at the corner of Vine Street and Grove Street NW, Decatur, Alabama. It still stands with the original cornerstone noting Rayfield as the architect.

Green Liberty Baptist Church was constructed circa 1914 for $3,000. It stands at the corner of Omega Street and 4th Avenue South in Birmingham, Alabama, bearing the original cornerstone with Rayfield's name.

Harmony Baptist Church was constructed in 1924 at the address of 527 42nd Place North, Birmingham, Alabama, for $25,000. The white marker in the center of the building is the original cornerstone announcing Rayfield as the architect.

Hunter's Chapel AME Zion Church was constructed in 1910, a renovation of the original 1881 building. The church is located at the corner of 11th Street and 22nd Avenue, Tuscaloosa, Alabama, and cost $8,000.

Kannapolis Presbyterian Church was built in 1923 at the intersection of West Avenue and C Street in Kannapolis, North Carolina, costing $60,000. It has since been demolished. Courtesy of Kannapolis Presbyterian.

King Memorial ME Church was constructed in 1908 at the address of 427 LaFayette Street in Decatur, Alabama. This building, along with the Sunday School building, cost $6,000. They have since been demolished.

Macedonia Seventeenth Street Baptist Church was constructed circa 1918 at the address of 17th Street North, Birmingham, Alabama. At the time it cost $10,000 and has since been demolished. Courtesy of Macedonia Baptist.

Marlinton Presbyterian Church was constructed circa 1915 at a cost of $10,000. It is located at 815 2nd Avenue, Marlinton, West Virginia. Courtesy of Marlinton Presbyterian.

Morning Pilgrim, later renamed 23rd Street Baptist, was built in 1908 at the address of 331 23rd Street South, Birmingham, Alabama, at a cost of $6,000.

Morning Star Baptist Church was built in 1920 at the address of 614 South Jackson Street, Demopolis, Alabama.

Mt. Ararat Baptist Church was constructed in 1927 at the address of 120 Slayden Avenue, Ensley, Alabama.

Mt. Gilead Baptist Church was built in 1912 at the address of 600 Grove Street, Fort Worth, Texas. Courtesy of Mt. Gilead Baptist.

Mt. Pilgrim Baptist Church was constructed in 1916 at 410 Clark Street, Milton, Florida, for $5,000. Photo by George Knight.

Mt. Zion Baptist Church was erected in 1914 at 528 W. Jackson Street, Pensacola, Florida. Photo by Delora Lightsey.

New Zion Baptist Church was originally built in 1911 at the address of 1026 24th Street North, Bessemer, Alabama. Since then the church has been rebuilt according to W. A. Rayfield's original plan. The original building cost $5,000.

Providence Baptist Church was constructed circa 1930 in Laurel, Mississippi. Photo by Sue Lightsey.

Roanoke Baptist Church was constructed circa 1914 for $25,000 at the address of 315 Whittington Avenue, Hot Springs, Arkansas. It has since been demolished. Courtesy of Roanoke Baptist.

Rocky Springs Presbyterian Church was constructed circa 1919 for a cost of $20,000 at the address of 933 Rocky Springs Church Road, Laurens, South Carolina.

St. Francis Xavier's Catholic Church was constructed circa 1915 for $7,000 at the address of 912 7th Street, Moundsville, West Virginia.

St. James Baptist Church was constructed in 1914 at the address of 1100 6th Avenue North in Birmingham, Alabama. It has since been demolished and the congregation has moved to 1200 20th Street North where they mounted the original cornerstone on the new church. Courtesy of St. James Baptist.

St. John AME Institutional Church was built in 1923 for $107,000 at the corner of 7th Avenue North and 15th Street North in Birmingham, Alabama. It was supposed to have twenty classrooms, a swimming pool, kitchen, dining room, library, lecture room, and a rooftop garden. It was demolished in 1971.

St. John Baptist Church was constructed circa 1918 at the address of 1919 Allen Street in Dallas, Texas, for $10,000. It included a hospital and film-showing equipment. It has since been demolished.

St. Luke AME was constructed circa 1917 for $3,000 at the address of 2800 22nd Avenue North in Birmingham, Alabama.

St. Paul Baptist Church was constructed circa 1909 at the address of 1404 South Georgia Street in Pine Bluff, Arkansas, for a cost of $27,000.

Sardis Baptist Church was constructed circa 1915 at the address of 1240 4th Street North, Birmingham, Alabama, for $7,000.

Second Baptist Church was constructed circa 1923 at the address of 1205 M. L. Cooper Drive in Waco, Texas, for $100,000. Courtesy of Second Baptist.

Sixteenth Street Baptist Church was built in 1909 on the corner of 16th Street North and 6th Avenue North in Birmingham, Alabama. It was the site of a bombing during the civil rights movement and stands today in its original form except for the repairs made after the bombing.

Sixteenth Street Baptist Church made a contract with Windham Brothers Construction Co. for the erection of a 70′ x 116′ brick and stone edifice costing $43,000. This 24′ x 70′ parsonage was included. Photo by Ellison Graham.

Sixth Avenue Baptist Church was constructed in 1910 for $30,000 at the address of 1521 F Street, Ensley, Alabama. It has since been demolished.

South Elyton Baptist Church was announced in 1929 to be built at the corner of Avenue A and 1st Street for $30,000. However, it was not built until the 1940s at the address of 100 1st Street South, Birmingham, Alabama.

32nd Street Baptist Church was constructed in 1924 at the address of 518 32nd Street South, Birmingham, Alabama. It still stands with its original cornerstone.

Trinity Baptist Church was constructed in 1908 for $15,000 at the address 526 4th Avenue North, Birmingham, Alabama.

Trinity ME Church, now Trinity United Methodist Church, was constructed circa 1915 at the address 122 Grand Avenue, Cumberland, Maryland. Courtesy of Trinity United Methodist.

Vestal ME Church was constructed circa 1925 for $35,000 at the address of 115 Ogle Avenue in Knoxville, Tennessee.

Weeping Mary Baptist Church was constructed circa 1930 for $30,000 at the corner of 20th Street and T. Y. Rogers Jr. Avenue in Tuscaloosa, Alabama.

3 Rayfield as School Architect

W. A. RAYFIELD & COMPANY
SCHOOL ARCHITECTS

BIRMINGHAM, ALA.

Rayfield did not use the same "Going to Build?" approach with schools as he did with homes and churches. For Rayfield, schools were an entirely different market and had to be approached in a different way. Instead of advertising, he acquired clients through his connections with the Methodist Church, the Freedmen's Aid Society, and the National Baptist Association. Rayfield did, however, create a *Book of Designs for Schools* to show clients samples of his work. He even drew sample designs of classrooms and included advertisements for blackboards, desks, and playgrounds in his *The School.*

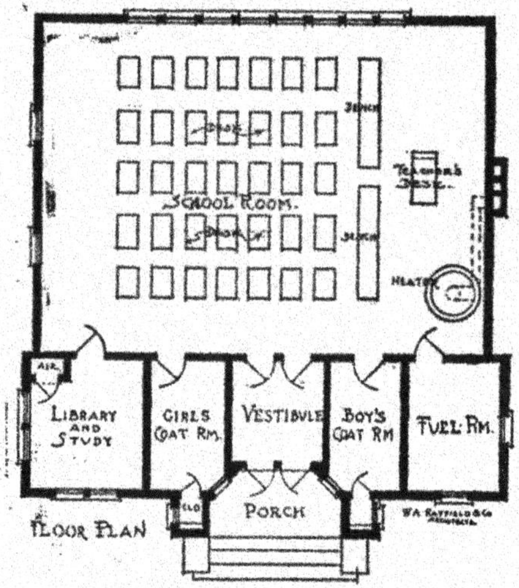

SPECIAL SCHOOL PLANS

We make a specialty of schools. Any individual ideas, we should be glad to co-operate with you and develop your plans. The cost is nominal for this class of work, two (2) per cent for plans and specifications complete.

The quotation Rayfield inscribed on the blackboard says: "Great is the function of the common school in our civilization and blessed is he who improves it." —Harris.

The Birmingham Baptist College Dormitory was constructed circa 1919 at the address of 630 Ishkooda Road SW in Birmingham, Alabama. It cost $12,000 and has since been destroyed.

Brainerd Hall, the main building of Central Alabama Institute, was built circa 1904 in Mason City, Alabama, now in the middle of Birmingham. It has since been demolished. Rayfield designed not only this building but also almost all the others as well as the landscape at Central Alabama Institute for a cost of $42,500.

The library of Gilbert Academy was constructed in the late 1800s in Baldwin, Louisiana. The Academy later moved to New Orleans and the library has since been demolished. Courtesy of Freedmen's Aid Society Records, Folder 525, Atlanta University Center, Robert W. Woodruff Library.

Hudson Negro School was constructed circa 1921 at the corner of 37th Street and 33rd Avenue in Birmingham, Alabama. Photo courtesy of the *Alabama School Journal.*

Calhoun Hall at Hungerford Industrial School was constructed in 1907 in Eatonville, Florida. The building has since been demolished.

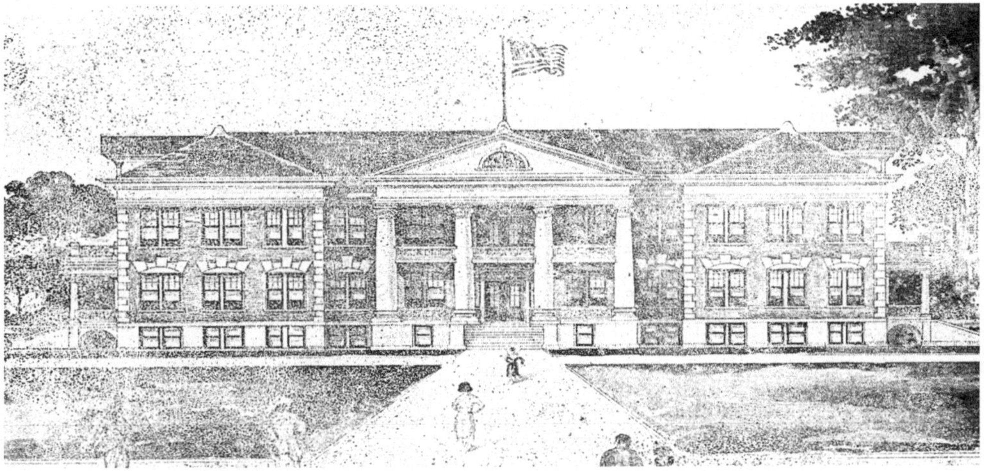

The construction of Male and Female College in Hopkinsville, Kentucky, was announced in 1920 and was to cost $50,000, but due to financial problems Rayfield's school plan was never used.

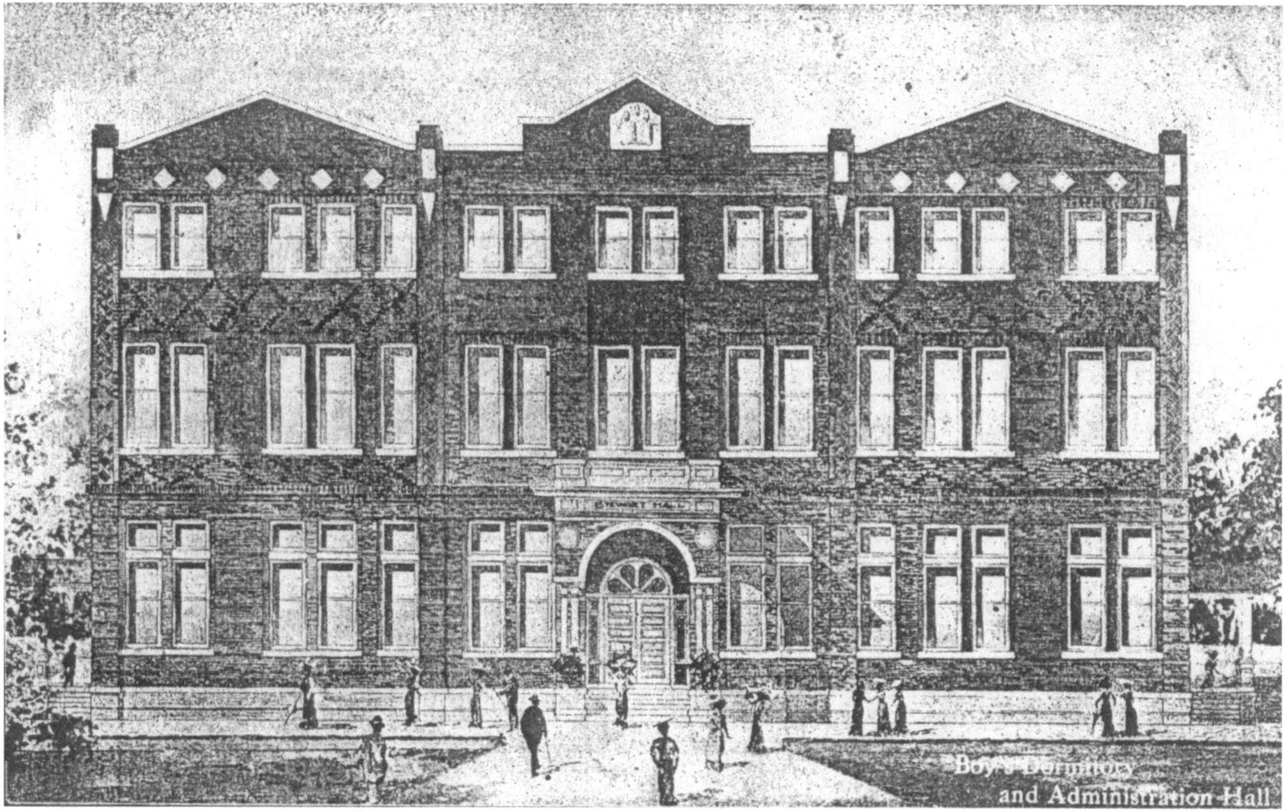

Stewart Hall of Miles College was constructed in 1911 at the address of 5500 Myron Massey Boulevard. The Hall was both an administration building and a boy's dormitory. It has since been demolished.

Williams Hall of Miles College was built in 1907 at the address 5500 Myron Massey Boulevard in Fairfield, Alabama. It was damaged by lightning and the tower and top floor had to be rebuilt. It otherwise remains in its original form.

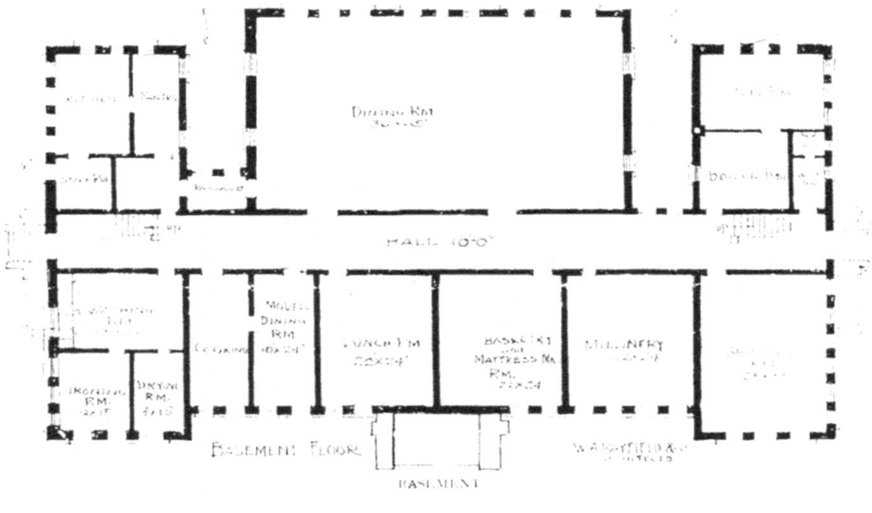

The Roosevelt Memorial School for Girls was built in 1919 according to this floor plan and illustration. It was constructed at the corner of Walker Street and 11th Avenue in Birmingham, Alabama, for $50,000. It has since been demolished. Courtesy of the Freedmen's Aid Archives.

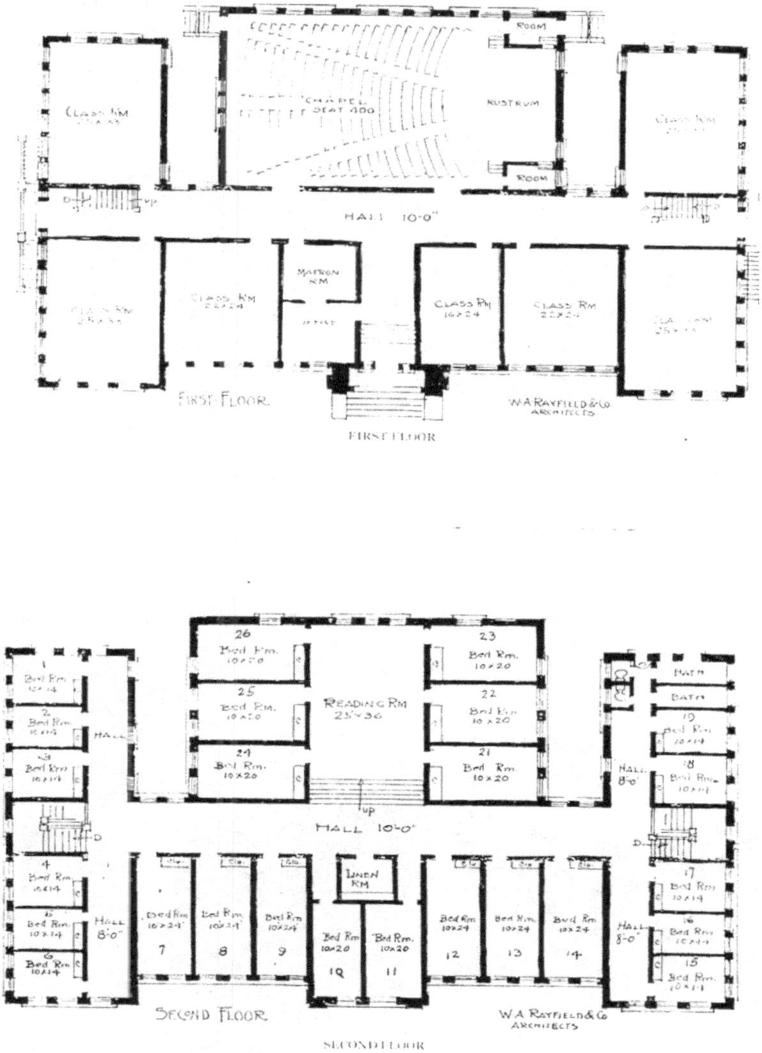

The Roosevelt Memorial School for Girls was built with a dormitory on the second floor ard classrooms on the first. Courtesy of the Freedmen's Aid Archives.

Thomas-Pettiford Negro School was constructed circa 1921 for $50,000.

Thomas-Pettiford Negro School still stands at the address of 3420 2nd Avenue North in Birmingham, Alabama, now headquarters for the Jimmie Hale Mission. Photo by Ellison Graham.

A three-story dormitory for Tuggle Institute was constructed circa 1908 at the address of 412 12th Court North in Birmingham, Alabama. It has since been demolished.

West Alabama Normal and Industrial Institute was constructed in 1912 in Geiger, Alabama, for a cost of $15,000.

4 Rayfield's Miscellaneous Architecture

Rayfield also created business establishments, apartments, theaters, office buildings, and even barns. He designed stores and storefronts of many different styles, catering to every need

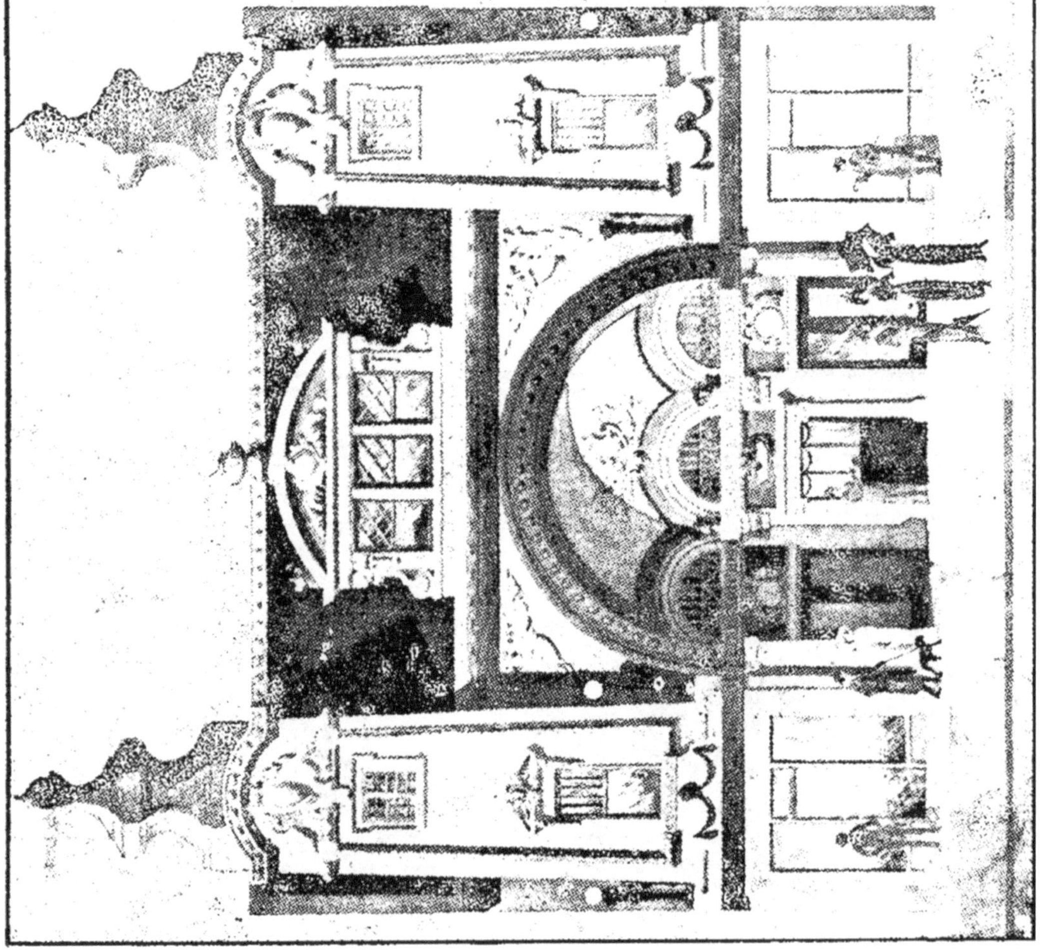

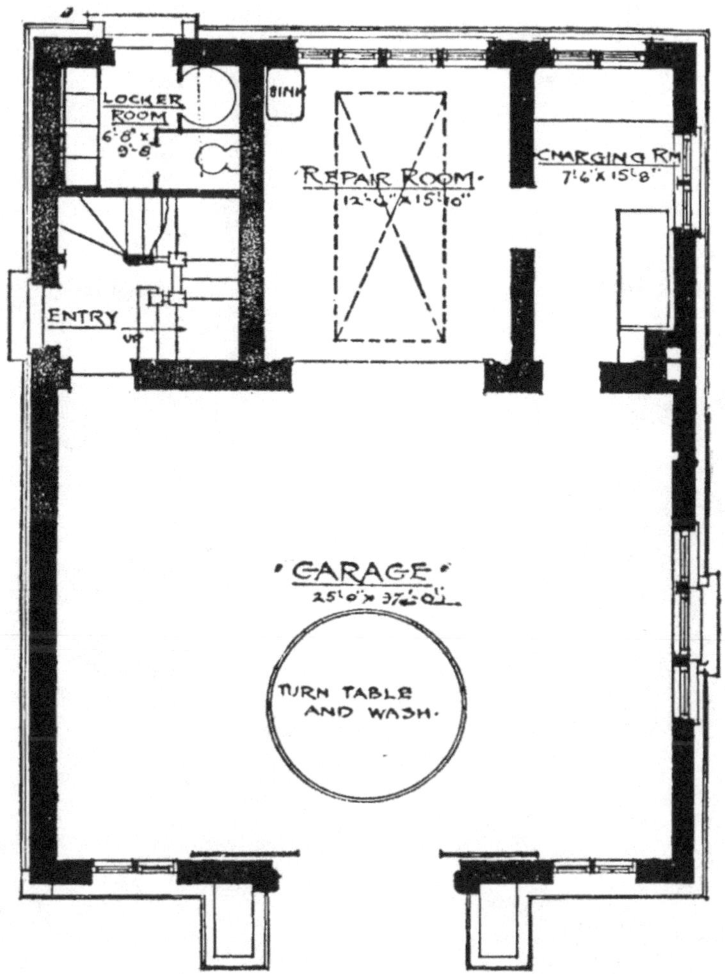
LOCKER ROOM
6'-8" x 9'-8"
SINK
REPAIR ROOM
CHARGING RM
7'-6" x 15'-8"
ENTRY
UP
GARAGE
TURN TABLE AND WASH

Rayfield also advertised for fraternal associations. He built Pythian Temples in both Alabama and Georgia.

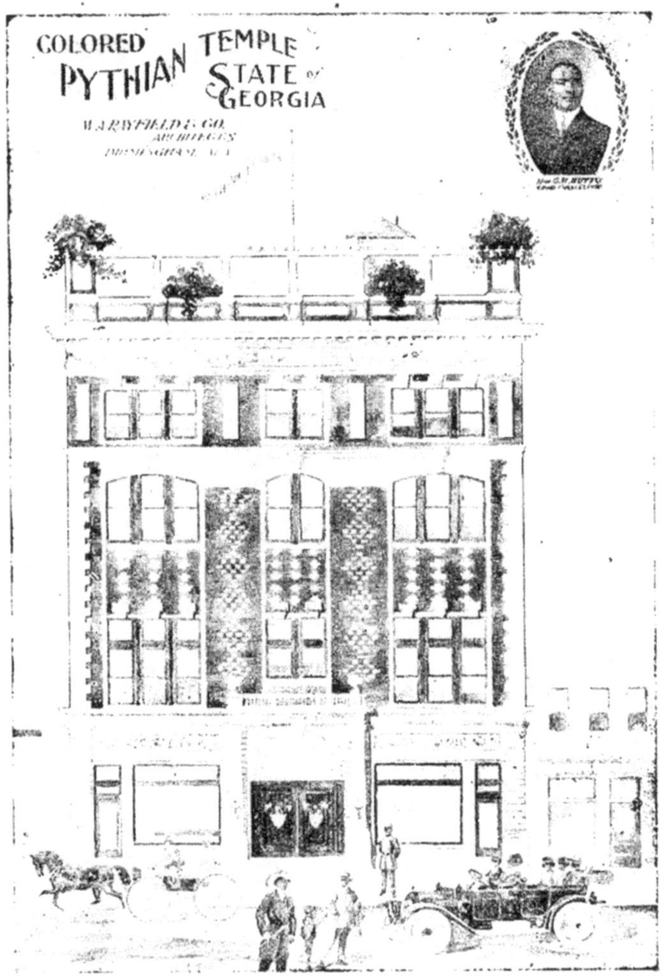

Rayfield also advertised his services as a barn architect, although no Rayfield barns are currently known to exist.

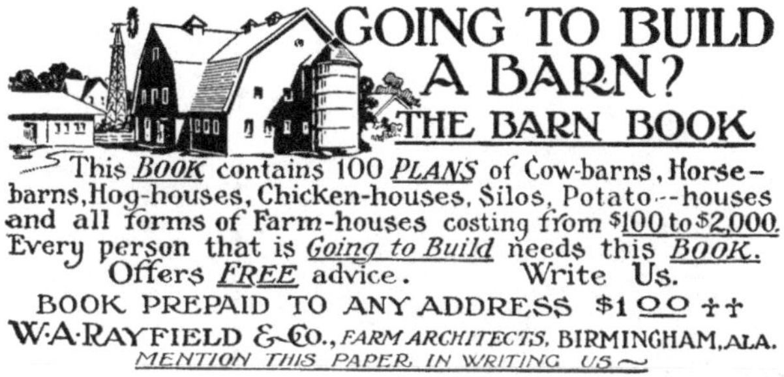

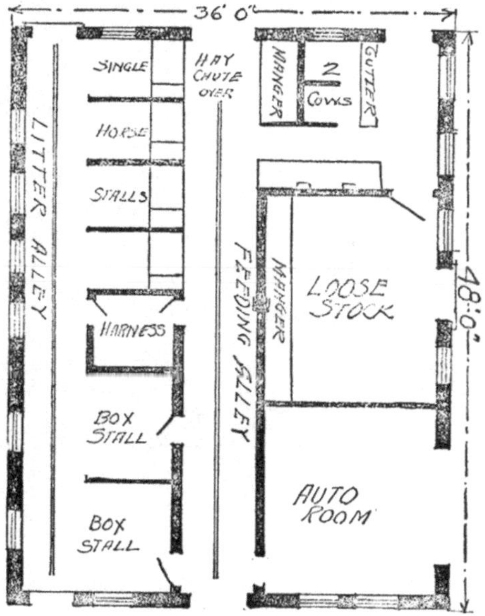

The six-story brick building is the Alabama Penny Prudential Savings Bank constructed in 1910. It later became the Pythian Temple Building and still stands at 310 18th Street North in Birmingham, Alabama.

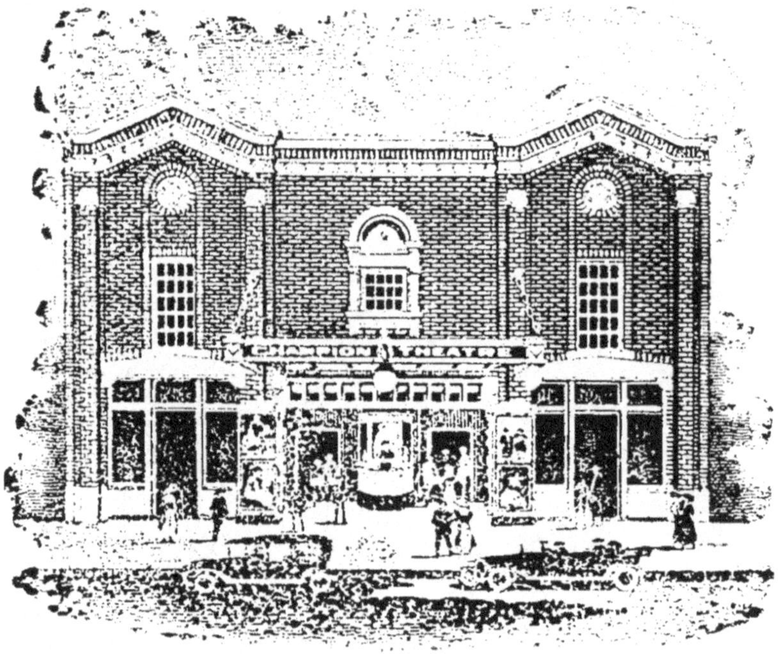

One of several, this Champion Theatre was constructed circa 1914 at the address of 306 18th Street North, adjacent to the Pythian Temple. At the time, construction cost $10,000. It has since been demolished.

This Champion Theatre was constructed circa 1927 at the address of 212 18th Street North for $25,000 and has since been demolished.

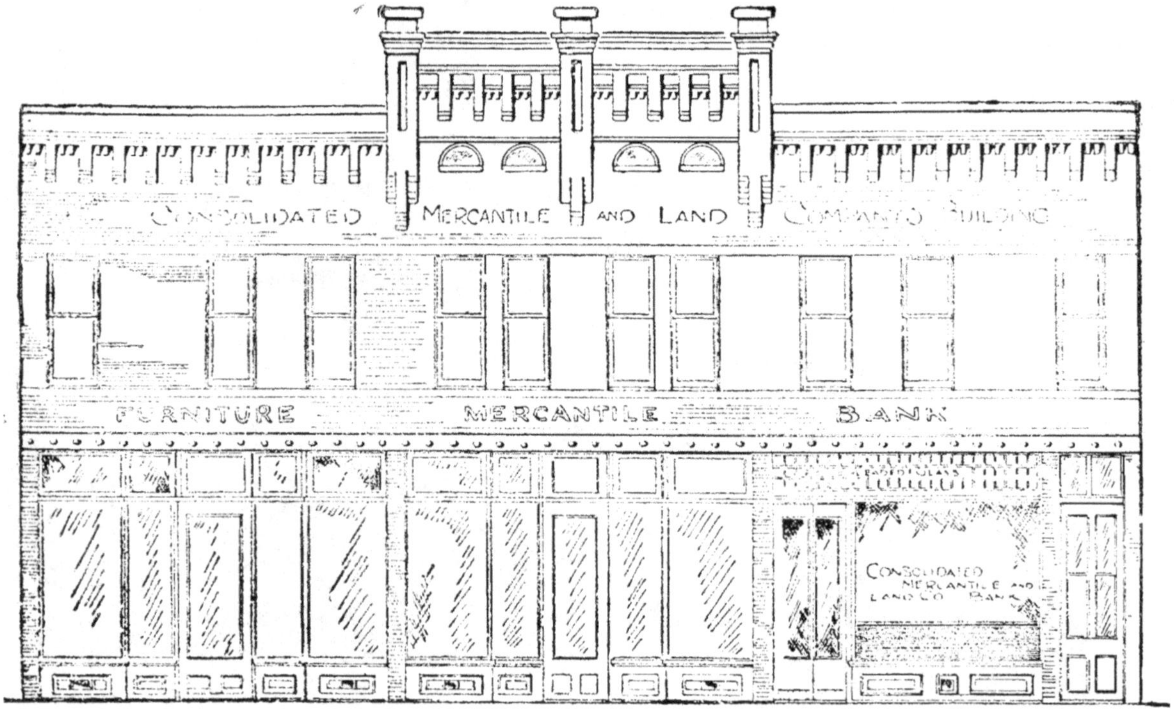

Consolidated Mercantile and Land Company was probably constructed in the neighborhood of Wylam in Birmingham, Alabama, in the early 1900s.

The Dunbar Hotel was constructed circa 1913 and still stands at the address of 1701 4th Avenue North in Birmingham, Alabama. Originally a high-class hotel, it is today the headquarters for Urban Impact, Inc., the Historical Fourth Avenue Visitors and Information Center. Photo by Ellison Graham.

The building of Echols & Strong Undertakers was constructed in 1910 at the address of 400 15th Street North in Birmingham, Alabama.

In 1911 Edgemont Cemetery Company contracted Rayfield to construct an entranceway that would cost $15,000. Its status is unknown.

Dr. Gordon's Indian Herb Drug Company office and store was constructed in 1911 at the address of 1023 3rd Avenue North in Birmingham, Alabama, at a cost of $8,000. It has since been demolished.

The office building of U. G. Mason was constructed circa 1908.

The U. G. Mason building stands today as the First National Mortgage building, at 1717 3rd Avenue North in Birmingham, Alabama.

O.K. French Cleaners was constructed circa 1908 at the address of 1705 4th Avenue North, Birmingham, Alabama. The building has hosted numerous businesses since its construction. It now stands as the Green Acres café. Photo by Ellison Graham.

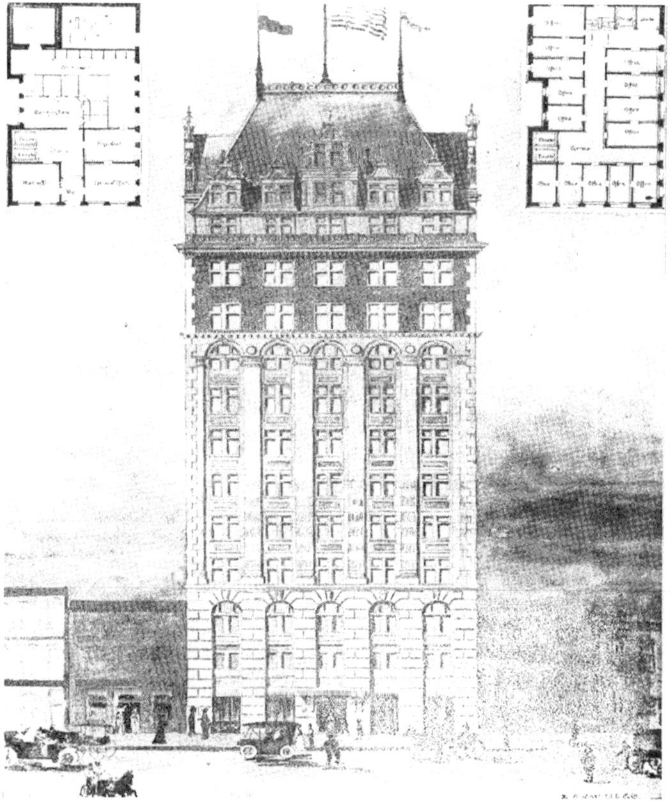

The Trinity Building was one of Rayfield's commercial buildings constructed in Africa.

Appendix 1

A List of Known Rayfield Structures

State (Country)	City	Plan Date	Building Name	Building Type
Liberia	Mt. Coffee	Dec. 22, 1923	AME Zion Church (4 buildings)	Church
Liberia?	Monrovia?	Unknown	Trinity Building	Commercial
Alabama	Anniston	Apr. 1, 1909	Mt. Olive Baptist	Church
Alabama	Anniston	Feb. 4, 1915	Hudson, W. H.	Residence
Alabama	Anniston	July 13, 1916	Mt. Olive Baptist	Church
Alabama	Attalla	Apr. 1, 1909	Mt. Zion Baptist Church Edifice	Church
Alabama	Bessemer	Jan. 26, 1911	Allen Temple AME	Church
Alabama	Bessemer	Mar. 9, 1911	New Zion Baptist	Church
Alabama	Bessemer	July 18, 1912	Grand Benevolent Association—Lodge Building	Fraternal
Alabama	Bessemer	Dec. 19, 1912	Bessemer Normal and Industrial	School
Alabama	Bessemer	July 23, 1914	Beulah Baptist	Church
Alabama	Bessemer	June 21, 1917	Beulah Baptist	Church
Alabama	Bessemer	June 27, 1918	First Baptist	Church

State (Country)	City	Plan Date	Building Name	Building Type
Alabama	Bessemer	Jan. 10, 1929	Mt. Olive Baptist Church	Church
Alabama	Birmingham	1908	Brown, E. A., Attorney	Residence
Alabama	Birmingham	Feb. 13, 1908	Brown, A. M.	Residence
Alabama	Birmingham	Feb. 27, 1908	New Hope Baptist	Church
Alabama	Birmingham	Feb. 27, 1908	Tuggle Institute Dormitory	School
Alabama	Birmingham	Mar. 12, 1908	King's Memorial United Methodist	Church
Alabama	Birmingham	Mar. 19, 1908	Sixteenth Street Tabernacle	Church
Alabama	Birmingham	Apr. 1, 1908	Butler, F. E.	Residence
Alabama	Birmingham	Apr. 1, 1908	Hillie, E. W.—Bungalow	Residence
Alabama	Birmingham	Apr. 1, 1908	Pettiford, W. R.	Residence
Alabama	Birmingham	July 16, 1908	Morning Pilgrim Baptist	Church
Alabama	Birmingham	July 16, 1908	Sixth Avenue Baptist	Church
Alabama	Birmingham	Dec. 3, 1908	Trinity Baptist	Church
Alabama	Birmingham	Jan. 14, 1909	Sixteenth Street Baptist	Church
Alabama	Birmingham	Jan. 14, 1909	Sixteenth Street Baptist—Pastorium	Pastorium
Alabama	Birmingham	Mar. 18, 1909	Butler, F. E.	Residence
Alabama	Birmingham	Mar. 18, 1909	Byrd, H. F.	Residence
Alabama	Birmingham	Mar. 18, 1909	Elk's Lodge	Fraternal
Alabama	Birmingham	Mar. 18, 1909	Richards, W. C.—Office and Store	Commercial

State (Country)	City	Plan Date	Building Name	Building Type
Alabama	Birmingham	Apr. 1, 1909	Townsend	Residence
Alabama	Birmingham	July 22, 1909	First Baptist (Colored)	Church
Alabama	Birmingham	Jan. 20, 1910	Johnson, B. F.	Residence
Alabama	Birmingham	Jan. 20, 1910	Reid, R.	Residence
Alabama	Birmingham	June 9, 1910	Cable, C. T.	Residence
Alabama	Birmingham	June 9, 1910	Echols & Strong	Funeral Home
Alabama	Birmingham	June 9, 1910	Jones, J. H.	Commercial
Alabama	Birmingham	June 9, 1910	Mason, U. G., Doctor—8 Stores	Commercial
Alabama	Birmingham	June 23, 1910	Prudential Savings Bank	Commercial
Alabama	Birmingham	June 23, 1910	St. Mark's Academic and Industrial Institute—3 Buildings	School
Alabama	Birmingham	Mar. 9, 1911	Edgemont Cemetery Company—Chapel Gate	Commercial
Alabama	Birmingham	July 27, 1911	Birmingham Baptist College	College
Alabama	Birmingham	July 27, 1911	Gordon Doctor/Indian Herb Drug Company	Commercial
Alabama	Birmingham	Oct. 21, 1911	Stewart, G. W.	Residence
Alabama	Birmingham	Feb. 22, 1912	Bernstedo, R.	Residence
Alabama	Birmingham	July 18, 1912	Fisher, C. L., Doctor	Residence
Alabama	Birmingham	Aug. 15, 1912	Jackson, J. S., Doctor	Residence
Alabama	Birmingham	Aug. 15, 1912	Montgomery, W. M.	Residence
Alabama	Birmingham	Aug. 29, 1912	Miles, Mrs. W. M.	Residence

State (Country)	City	Plan Date	Building Name	Building Type
Alabama	Birmingham	1914	St. James Baptist	Church
Alabama	Birmingham	1914	South Avondale Baptist	Church
Alabama	Birmingham	Feb. 12, 1914	Blount, R. A.	Residence
Alabama	Birmingham	Feb. 19, 1914	St. John's Institutional AME	Church
Alabama	Birmingham	Feb. 26, 1914	Jonas Schwab—Apartments	Multi-Residence
Alabama	Birmingham	Mar. 26, 1914	Jackson, J. S., Doctor—Store and Apartments	Commercial
Alabama	Birmingham	May 7, 1914	Champion Theater #2	Commercial
Alabama	Birmingham	May 7, 1914	Mohan Realty Company—Apartments	Multi-Residence
Alabama	Birmingham	May 14, 1914	Jonas Schwab—Alpha Flats—Apartments	Multi-Residence
Alabama	Birmingham	May 14, 1914	Story, C. P.—Flats—5 Family—Apartments	Multi-Residence
Alabama	Birmingham	June 4, 1914	Streit Realty Apartments	Multi-Residence
Alabama	Birmingham	June 18, 1914	Tinker, W. E.	Residence
Alabama	Birmingham	July 9, 1914	CME Publishing Company	Commercial
Alabama	Birmingham	July 9, 1914	(unidentified) Baptist Church	Church
Alabama	Birmingham	July 23, 1914	Ellison, C. D.	Residence
Alabama	Birmingham	Sept. 3, 1914	Anderson, B. J., Doctor	Residence
Alabama	Birmingham	Sept. 3, 1914	Randall, P. J. Clyde	Residence
Alabama	Birmingham	Oct. 29, 1914	Thurgood Memorial CME	Church
Alabama	Birmingham	Nov. 5, 1914	Ellis, N. B.	Residence

State (Country)	City	Plan Date	Building Name	Building Type
Alabama	Birmingham	Nov. 19, 1914	Broad Street Baptist	Church
Alabama	Birmingham	Nov. 19, 1914	Green Liberty Baptist	Church
Alabama	Birmingham	Nov. 26, 1914	Consolidated Amusement Company	Commercial
Alabama	Birmingham	Dec. 2, 1914	Jonas Schwab—Apartments	Multi-Residence
Alabama	Birmingham	Dec. 17, 1914	White, A.	Residence
Alabama	Birmingham	June 24, 1915	Edwards, P. M.	Residence
Alabama	Birmingham	Sept. 9, 1915	Diffay, J. O.—Store	Commercial
Alabama	Birmingham	Sept. 9, 1915	Johnson, W. B.—Store	Commercial
Alabama	Birmingham	Sept. 9, 1915	Lively Hope Church, Pratt City	Church
Alabama	Birmingham	Sept. 9, 1915	Sardis Baptist	Church
Alabama	Birmingham	Nov. 18, 1915	Forty-Fifth Street Baptist	Church
Alabama	Birmingham	Feb. 10, 1916	Snider, W. O.—3 Stores	Commercial
Alabama	Birmingham	May 4, 1916	Second Baptist	Church
Alabama	Birmingham	May 10, 1917	St. Luke AME	Church
Alabama	Birmingham	June 21, 1917	Shanks, M. B., Mrs.—6 Houses	Residence
Alabama	Birmingham	Nov. 15, 1917	Savoy Theatre	Commercial
Alabama	Birmingham	Apr. 18, 1918	Macedonia Baptist	Church
Alabama	Birmingham	Apr. 18, 1918	Seventeenth Street Baptist	Church
Alabama	Birmingham	Aug. 8, 1918	First Baptist, East Irondale	Church

State (Country)	City	Plan Date	Building Name	Building Type
Alabama	Birmingham	Aug. 29, 1918	Payne Chapel AME	Church
Alabama	Birmingham	Dec. 12, 1918	McCombs Chapel, Pratt City	Church
Alabama	Birmingham	Feb. 6, 1919	St. James Methodist	Church
Alabama	Birmingham	May 8, 1919	Roosevelt Memorial School for Girls	School
Alabama	Birmingham	July 10, 1919	First Baptist, Ensley	Church
Alabama	Birmingham	July 24, 1919	Gaines Methodist	Church
Alabama	Birmingham	Nov. 27, 1919	Birmingham Baptist College—Dormitory	College
Alabama	Birmingham	Nov. 27, 1919	Madam Christy	Residence
Alabama	Birmingham	Aug. 19, 1920	Friendship Baptist	Church
Alabama	Birmingham	July 4, 1921	St. Paul ME	Church
Alabama	Birmingham	Nov. 17, 1921	Hudson (Negro)	School
Alabama	Birmingham	Nov. 17, 1921	Thomas / Pettiford (Thomas School)	School
Alabama	Birmingham	Nov. 24, 1921	Harmony Baptist	Church
Alabama	Birmingham	Nov. 24, 1921	Shiloh Baptist	Church
Alabama	Birmingham	Dec. 22, 1923	Washington Public (Plate 001)	School
Alabama	Birmingham	Dec. 22, 1923	Windham, T. C., Contractor, The Mansion	Residence
Alabama	Birmingham	1924	Thirty-Second Street Baptist	Church
Alabama	Birmingham	1926	Dobbins, A. G.	Residence
Alabama	Birmingham	1926	Brown, R. T., Bishop	Residence

State (Country)	City	Plan Date	Building Name	Building Type
Alabama	Birmingham	July 23, 1927	Metropolitan AME	Church
Alabama	Birmingham	July 28, 1927	Metropolitan AME	Church
Alabama	Birmingham	Apr. 12, 1928	Spencer, W. F., Roebuck Springs	Residence
Alabama	Birmingham	Apr. 12, 1928	Temple Baptist	Church
Alabama	Birmingham	May 3, 1928	Harris, T. L.	Residence
Alabama	Birmingham	May 3, 1928	Phillips Home Building Company	Commercial
Alabama	Birmingham	May 3, 1928	Shady Grove Baptist	Church
Alabama	Birmingham	May 3, 1928	Trinity CME, Pratt City	Church
Alabama	Birmingham	July 26, 1928	Twenty-Fifth Avenue Baptist	Church
Alabama	Birmingham	Aug. 30, 1928	Echols & Story—Apartments	Commercial
Alabama	Birmingham	June 20, 1929	Forty-Fifth Street Baptist	Church
Alabama	Birmingham	July 18, 1929	Elyton Baptist	Church
Alabama	Birmingham	July 18, 1929	Twenty-Fifth Avenue Baptist	Church
Alabama	Birmingham	Unknown	Black, W. H.	Residence
Alabama	Birmingham	Unknown	Central Alabama Institute—Administration Building	College
Alabama	Birmingham	Unknown	Champion Theater #1	Commercial
Alabama	Birmingham	Unknown	Coar, John Moses	Residence
Alabama	Birmingham	Unknown	Commons, John W.	Residence
Alabama	Birmingham	Unknown	Consolidated Merchantile Company	Commercial

State (Country)	City	Plan Date	Building Name	Building Type
Alabama	Birmingham	Unknown	Davenport Harris Building	Commercial
Alabama	Birmingham	Unknown	Dunbar Hotel	Commercial
Alabama	Birmingham	Unknown	First Congregational Church	Church
Alabama	Birmingham	Unknown	Harriet Strong Undertaking Company	Commercial
Alabama	Birmingham	Unknown	Mabry, Charles T., Professor	Residence
Alabama	Birmingham	Unknown	Madam Clisby	Residence
Alabama	Birmingham	Unknown	Mason, U. G., Doctor	Residence
Alabama	Birmingham	Unknown	Mason, U. G.—Office Building	Commercial
Alabama	Birmingham	Unknown	Mt. Ararat Baptist	Church
Alabama	Birmingham	Unknown	O. K. French Cleaners	Commercial
Alabama	Birmingham	Unknown	Parker, Arthur H.	Residence
Alabama	Birmingham	Unknown	Pharrow, Robert E., Contractor	Residence
Alabama	Birmingham	Unknown	Pythian Temple	Fraternal
Alabama	Birmingham	Unknown	Rayfield, Wallace A., and Bessie	Residence
Alabama	Birmingham	Unknown	Rayfield, Wallace A., and Jennie	Residence
Alabama	Birmingham	Unknown	Seymour, R. W.	Residence
Alabama	Birmingham	Unknown	Smith, E. H., Esq.	Residence
Alabama	Birmingham	Unknown	Strawbridge, Fred H., Doctor	Residence
Alabama	Birmingham	Unknown	(unidentified) Residence Plate 143 The Argenta Bungalow	Residence

State (Country)	City	Plan Date	Building Name	Building Type
Alabama	Birmingham	Unknown	(unidentified) Residence Plate 145 The Birmingham Bungalow	Residence
Alabama	Birmingham	Unknown	(unidentified) Residence Plate 408/The Jennette Bungalow	Residence
Alabama	Birmingham	Unknown	Walton's Café	Commercial
Alabama	Brighton	May 14, 1914	Brighton First Baptist Church	Church
Alabama	Carbon Hill	Aug. 30, 1928	Lodge Building (unidentified)	Fraternal
Alabama	Cordova	Mar. 9, 1911	unidentified school	School
Alabama	Corona	Mar. 19, 1908	Corona Normal and Industrial—Dorm 2 Stories	School
Alabama	Dayton	June 24, 1915	First Baptist Church	Church
Alabama	Decatur	Dec. 3, 1908	King's Memorial United Methodist	Church
Alabama	Decatur	Mar. 4, 1926	Waymon Chapel AME	Church
Alabama	Decatur	Unknown	First Missionary Baptist	Church
Alabama	Demopolis	Aug. 10, 1911	New Zion Baptist—Edifice	Church
Alabama	Demopolis	1920	Morning Star Baptist	Church
Alabama	Dothan	Feb. 27, 1908	New Hope Baptist—Church Edifice	Church
Alabama	Fairfield	June 9, 1910	Miles College—Administration Building	College
Alabama	Fairfield	June 9, 1910	Miles College—Boy's Dormitory	College
Alabama	Fairfield	June 9, 1910	Miles College—Boy's Science Hall	College
Alabama	Fairfield	June 9, 1910	Miles College—Chapel and Hospital	College
Alabama	Fairfield	June 9, 1910	Miles College—Memorial Dormitory	College

State (Country)	City	Plan Date	Building Name	Building Type
Alabama	Fairfield	June 9, 1910	Miles College—Stewart Hall	College
Alabama	Fairfield	June 9, 1910	Miles College—Williams Hall	College
Alabama	Fairfield	Mar. 30, 1911	Miles College—Stewart Hall	College
Alabama	Fairfield	Unknown	Smith-Gaston	Residence
Alabama	Florence	Sept. 16, 1920	Baptist Church	Church
Alabama	Gadsden	July 2, 1908	Friendship Baptist Edifice	Church
Alabama	Geiger	July 18, 1912	West Alabama Normal and Industrial Institute	College
Alabama	Hobson City	Feb. 2, 1911	New Hope Baptist—Edifice	Church
Alabama	Huntsville	Jan. 23, 1913	Lakeside ME	Church
Alabama	Kowaliga	Aug. 5, 1909	Kowaliga Normal & Industrial—5 buildings	School
Alabama	Leeds	July 10, 1919	Hayward, W. F.	Commercial
Alabama	Linden	Apr. 15, 1915	First Baptist	Church
Alabama	Lineville	1913	Lineville Baptist	Church
Alabama	Mobile	Oct. 9, 1930	Stone Street Baptist	Church
Alabama	Montgomery	July 22, 1909	Scott, D. H. C., Doctor	Commercial
Alabama	Montgomery	Unknown	Day Street Baptist	Church
Alabama	Normal	Sept. 2, 1915	Alabama Agricultural and Mechanical College—2 dorms	College
Alabama	Notasulga	Unknown	Stevenson, W. S., Colonel	Residence
Alabama	Selma	July 14, 1910	Payne University—Dormitory	College

State (Country)	City	Plan Date	Building Name	Building Type
Alabama	Selma	July 14, 1910	Selma University—Foster Hall	College
Alabama	Selma	Oct. 6, 1910	Burwell, L. L., Doctor	Residence
Alabama	Selma	Oct. 6, 1910	Hudson, R. B.	Residence
Alabama	Selma	Oct. 21, 1911	Gilbert C. P., Doctor	Residence
Alabama	Selma	Dec. 12, 1918	Barnes, H. A.	Residence
Alabama	Selma	Feb. 6, 1919	Hudson, R. B.	Residence
Alabama	Selma	June 20, 1929	Alabama Baptist College Banks School of Music	College
Alabama	Sheffield	Jan. 31, 1918	Methodist Episcopal	Church
Alabama	Sylacauga	1914	First Baptist Church	Church
Alabama	Tuscaloosa	July 22, 1909	Hunter's Chapel AME Zion	Church
Alabama	Tuscaloosa	Aug. 10, 1911	St. Paul ME—Edifice	Church
Alabama	Tuscaloosa	Feb. 12, 1914	Baileys Tabernacle CME	Church
Alabama	Tuscaloosa	Feb. 19, 1914	Baileys Tabernacle CME	Church
Alabama	Tuscaloosa	July 18, 1929	Weeping Mary Baptist	Church
Alabama	Tuscaloosa	June 5, 1930	Weeping Mary Baptist	Church
Alabama	Tuskegee	Jan. 28, 1915	Tuskegee N. and I. Institute—(25 Sch. For St.)	College
Alabama	Tuskegee	Feb. 6, 1919	Tuskegee N. and I. Institute, Slater—Armstrong Trades Building	College
Arkansas	Batesville	Sept. 9, 1915	St. Paul Episcopal Church	Church
Arkansas	England	July 10, 1919	First Baptist	Church

State (Country)	City	Plan Date	Building Name	Building Type
Arkansas	Harrison	Apr. 26, 1917	Mitchell, F. R.	Residence
Arkansas	Harrison	Feb. 13, 1919	House (unidentified)	Residence
Arkansas	Harrison	Mar. 27, 1919	Mitchell, F. R.	Residence
Arkansas	Hot Springs	Oct. 22, 1914	Roanoke Baptist	Church
Arkansas	Little Rock	Sept. 25, 1930	First Baptist—Highland Park	Church
Arkansas	Magnolia	May 7, 1914	First Baptist	Church
Arkansas	Monticello	Jan. 26, 1911	New Zion AME, Edifice	Church
Arkansas	Newell	Jan. 14, 1915	First Baptist	Church
Arkansas	Pine Bluff	Jan. 14, 1909	St. Paul Baptist	Church
Arkansas	Pine Bluff	Apr. 1, 1909	St. Paul Baptist, Edifice	Church
Arkansas	Pine Bluff	Oct. 22, 1914	Grace Temple Baptist	Church
Arkansas	Postelle	Feb. 2, 1911	AME, Edifice	Church
Arkansas	Stamp	June 24, 1915	(unidentified) Church (Richard, A.—Pastor)	Church
Arkansas	Waldron	Aug. 23, 1917	Waldron Baptist	Church
Arkansas	Waldron	Sept. 6, 1917	Waldron Baptist Church and S.S.	Church
Arkansas	Waldron	Feb. 28, 1918	Waldron Baptist Church and S.S.	Church
Arkansas	Warren	Apr. 1, 1920	Walters Institute—Girls Dormitory	School
Arkansas	Warren	Feb. 24, 1921	Walters Institute—Girls Dormitory	School
Florida	Clearwater	May 18, 1922	St. Mathew's First Baptist	Church

State (Country)	City	Plan Date	Building Name	Building Type
Florida	Daytona	Sept. 3, 1914	Mt. Bethel Baptist	Church
Florida	Eatonville	Unknown	Hungerford School—Calhoun Hall	School
Florida	Jacksonville	Dec. 2, 1920	First Christian	Church
Florida	Jacksonville	Dec. 2, 1920	Tabernacle Institutional Baptist	Church
Florida	Milton	Apr. 20, 1916	Mt. Pilgrim Baptist	Church
Florida	Ocala	Oct. 22, 1914	Mt. Moriah Baptist	Church
Florida	Ocala	Apr. 27, 1922	Mt. Moriah Baptist	Church
Florida	Ocala	May 4, 1922	Mt. Moriah Baptist	Church
Florida	Pensacola	Feb. 5, 1914	Mt. Zion Baptist	Church
Florida	Tampa	Mar. 2, 1922	Beulah Baptist Church	Church
Florida	Wewahitchka	Feb. 2, 1911	AME, Church Edifice	Church
Florida	Winter Haven	Oct. 28, 1915	First Baptist	Church
Georgia		Jan. 14, 1909	Pythian New Castle Hall	Fraternal
Georgia	Americus	Dec. 9, 1915	Lee Street ME	Church
Georgia	Atlanta	May 8, 1919	Hotel (unidentified)	Commercial
Georgia	Fitzgerald	Feb. 5, 1914	Ben Hill County Public High School	School
Georgia	Griffin	Jan. 14, 1909	Mt. Zion Baptist Church Edifice	Church
Georgia	Macon	Mar. 30, 1911	Pythian Temple (colored)	Fraternal
Georgia	Macon	Apr. 11, 1912	Pythian Grand Lodge Building	Fraternal

State (Country)	City	Plan Date	Building Name	Building Type
Georgia	Macon	Mar. 26, 1914	(unidentified) Theater	Commercial
Georgia	Macon	July 19, 1917	Hinton, J. C.	Residence
Georgia	Mauk	Jan. 26, 1911	AME Church Edifice	Church
Georgia	Savannah	Dec. 2, 1915	Methodist Church	Church
Georgia	Statesboro	Nov. 1, 1917	Van Buren Sanitarium	Medical
Georgia	Wiley	Feb. 6, 1919	Ashe, T. B.	Residence
Illinois	Chicago	Unknown	Ebenezer Baptist	Church
Kentucky	Augusta	Apr. 12, 1928	St. Paul Lutheran	Church
Kentucky	Burkesville	Dec. 2, 1915	Christian Church	Church
Kentucky	Covington	Oct. 14, 1915	First Baptist Church	Church
Kentucky	Cynthiana	Sept. 25, 1930	Macedonia Baptist	Church
Kentucky	Glendale	Apr. 20, 1916	First Baptist	Church
Kentucky	Harrodsburg	Apr. 15, 1915	First Baptist	Church
Kentucky	Hazard	Dec. 2, 1915	First Baptist	Church
Kentucky	Hopkinsville	Aug. 19, 1920	Kentucky M.&F. College	College
Kentucky	Lexington	July 15, 1915	First Baptist Church Sunday School Building	Church
Kentucky	Louisville	1910	Lampton Missionary Baptist	Church
Kentucky	Louisville	Apr. 25, 1918	Mt. Lebanon Baptist	Church
Kentucky	Louisville	Dec. 12, 1918	Mt. Lebanon Baptist	Church

State (Country)	City	Plan Date	Building Name	Building Type
Kentucky	Louisville	Feb. 27, 1919	Mt. Lebanon Church—Auditorium	Church
Kentucky	Louisville	Feb. 27, 1919	Mt. Lebanon Church—Sunday School Annex	Church
Kentucky	Mayfield	Mar. 27, 1919	School Building Graded	School
Kentucky	Middlesboro	Apr. 7, 1921	Mt. Moriah Baptist	Church
Kentucky	Somerset	1913	Somerset Baptist	Church
Louisiana	Baldwin	Unknown	Gilbert Academy—Library	College
Louisiana	Freeport	Dec. 22, 1923	Church of the Good Shepherd	Church
Louisiana	Lake Providence	July 10, 1919	Grace Episcopal	Church
Louisiana	Monroe	July 26, 1928	Zion Travelers Baptist	Church
Maryland	Baltimore	Dec. 22, 1923	Grace Evangelical Lutheran	Church
Maryland	Cumberland	Aug. 5, 1915	Trinity ME	Church
Maryland	Cumberland	Unknown	Trinity ME	Church
Mississippi	Brazil	Dec. 12, 1918	Johnson High School	School
Mississippi	Greenville	Oct. 10, 1930	St. Paul's Baptist	Church
Mississippi	Greenwood	Jan. 31, 1918	New Zion Baptist	Church
Mississippi	Hattiesburg	Mar. 19, 1925	True Light Baptist (Colored)	Church
Mississippi	Holly Springs	July 9, 1921	Rust College—McDonald Hall Renovation	College
Mississippi	Holly Springs	Nov. 5, 1923	Rust College—Science Hall	College
Mississippi	Jackson	Jan. 26, 1911	Atwood & McKissack—Store	Commercial

State (Country)	City	Plan Date	Building Name	Building Type
Mississippi	Jackson	Feb. 2, 1911	Atwood & McKissack—Store	Commercial
Mississippi	Laurel	Sept. 25, 1930	Providence Baptist	Church
Mississippi	Lexington	Nov. 5, 1914	Lebanon Baptist	Church
Mississippi	McComb	Apr. 15, 1915	First Baptist Sunday School Building	Church
Mississippi	Meridian	Unknown	Haven Institute and Conservatory Dormitory	College
Mississippi	Mound Bayou	May 15, 1916	Mound Bayou College	College
Mississippi	Oklona	May 1, 1919	Oklona Industrial College -Girls Trades Building	School
Mississippi	Utica	June 4, 1914	Utica Normal and Industrial Institute—Girl's Dormitory	School
Mississippi	Utica	June 4, 1914	Utica Normal & Industrial Institute—President's Home	School
Mississippi	Vicksburg	May 8, 1919	Heroden Baptist	Church
Missouri	Blue Springs	Dec. 9, 1915	First Baptist	Church
Missouri	Liberty	May 4, 1916	Chandler Baptist	Church
North Carolina	Concord	June 27, 1918	First Baptist	Church
North Carolina	Hendersonville	Jan. 10, 1929	Star of Bethel Baptist	Church
North Carolina	Holly Springs	Apr. 26, 1917	Holly Springs Baptist	Church
North Carolina	Kannapolis	Dec. 22, 1923	Kannapolis Presbyterian	Church
North Carolina	Morehead City	Apr. 18, 1918	St. Stephen's Methodist Episcopal	Church
North Carolina	Morehead City	June 19, 1918	St. Stephen's Methodist Episcopal	Church
North Carolina	Salisbury	June 18, 1914	Zion AME	Church

State (Country)	City	Plan Date	Building Name	Building Type
North Carolina	Salisbury	Apr. 20, 1916	First Congregational	Church
North Carolina	Wilmington	June 19, 1918	Hebron Baptist	Church
North Carolina	Wilmington	June 27, 1918	Ebenezer Baptist	Church
Ohio	Cincinnati	Dec. 22, 1923	Antioch Baptist	Church
Ohio	Cleveland	Dec. 22, 1923	St. James AME	Church
Oklahoma	Altus	Jan. 10, 1929	Macedonia Baptist	Church
Oklahoma	Boley	Dec. 12, 1918	(unidentified) Institute—Educational Building	School
Oklahoma	Chickasha	May 9, 1918	Methodist	Church
Oklahoma	Cleveland	Oct. 9, 1930	Baptist	Church
Oklahoma	Heavner	Apr. 26, 1917	First Baptist	Church
Oklahoma	Heavner	May 10, 1917	Baptist	Church
Oklahoma	Henryetta	July 23, 1914	Christian Science	Church
Oklahoma	Muskogee	Mar. 27, 1919	Shiloh Baptist	Church
Oklahoma	Oklahoma City	May 8, 1919	St. John's Baptist	Church
Oklahoma	Ponca City	Mar. 18, 1915	First Baptist	Church
Oklahoma	Tulsa	Mar. 21, 1918	First Baptist	Church
Oklahoma	Tulsa	June 19, 1918	First Baptist	Church
Oklahoma	White Oak	June 24, 1915	First Christian	Church
Pennsylvania	Allenton	Dec. 22, 1923	First Reform	Church

State (Country)	City	Plan Date	Building Name	Building Type
Pennsylvania	Pittsburgh	Dec. 22, 1923	Central Baptist	Church
South Carolina	Columbia	Jan. 4, 1912	AME	Church
South Carolina	Laurens	Nov. 27, 1919	Rocky Springs Presbyterian	Church
South Carolina	Spartanburg	Jan. 19, 1922	Trinity AME	Church
Tennessee	Chattanooga	May 13, 1915	Zion AME	Church
Tennessee	Memphis	June 19, 1918	Mt. Zion Baptist	Church
Tennessee	Vestal/Knoxville	Oct. 8, 1925	Vestal ME	Church
Texas	Alpine	Dec. 9, 1915	First Baptist	Church
Texas	Beaumont	June 4, 1914	Baptist	Church
Texas	Beaumont	July 15, 1915	East Mount Olive Baptist	Church
Texas	College Station	July 26, 1928	First Baptist	Church
Texas	Dallas	May 4, 1916	Macedonia Baptist	Church
Texas	Dallas	May 30, 1918	St. John's Institutional	Church
Texas	Denison	Apr. 15, 1915	Mt. Zion Baptist	Church
Texas	Fort Worth	Oct. 28, 1915	Methodist Episcopal	Church
Texas	Fort Worth	Unknown	Mt. Gilead Baptist	Church
Texas	Freeport	Aug. 19, 1920	Freeport Catholic	Church
Texas	Galveston	July 15, 1915	Avenue L Baptist	Church
Texas	Gonzales	Feb. 2, 1911	Mt. Pilgrim Baptist	Church

State (Country)	City	Plan Date	Building Name	Building Type
Texas	Houston	Mar. 26, 1914	Antioch Baptist	Church
Texas	Jacksboro	July 9, 1914	First Presbyterian	Church
Texas	Marshall	June 23, 1920	Wiley College—Coe Memorial Building	College
Texas	Orange	Mar. 26, 1914	Mt. Olive Baptist	Church
Texas	Palestine	July 23, 1914	Bethel ME	Church
Texas	San Angelo	Jan. 10, 1929	Emmanuel Episcopal	Church
Texas	San Antonio	Mar. 26, 1914	Bethel ME	Church
Texas	San Antonio	Mar. 26, 1914	Mt. Zion Baptist	Church
Texas	Seguin	Dec. 22, 1923	Guadalupe College—Building	College
Texas	Sulphur Springs	Feb. 25, 1915	Baptist	Church
Texas	Waco	Dec. 22, 1923	Second Baptist	Church
Texas	Waco	Unknown	(unidentified) Public School	School
Virginia	Portsmouth	Mar. 18, 1915	St. Thomas Baptist	Church
Virginia	Richmond	July 24, 1919	Mt. Olive Baptist	Church
Washington, DC		Oct. 3, 1914	(unidentified) School—Dormitory	School
West Virginia	Charleston	Oct. 14, 1915	First Church of Christ Scientist	Church
West Virginia	Hinton	Sept. 21, 1916	(unidentified) Church, Rives, J. J., Pastor	Church
West Virginia	Marlinton	June 3, 1915	Presbyterian	Church
West Virginia	Marlinton	June 15, 1922	ME Church South	Church

State (Country)	City	Plan Date	Building Name	Building Type
West Virginia	Marlinton	Dec. 22, 1923	First ME	Church
West Virginia	Moundsville	July 15, 1915	St. Francis Xavier Roman Catholic	Church
West Virginia	St. Albans	Dec. 12, 1918	St. Paul's Baptist	Church
West Virginia	St. Albans	Apr. 7, 1921	St. Paul's Baptist	Church

Appendix 2

Rayfield's Industrial Drawing Book

W. A. Rayfield's Industrial Drawing Book is a sixty-eight-page, 7″ x 9″ hardback book containing twenty-four drawings that illustrate the basic architectural drawing methods he used and taught. As the instructor of industrial drawing at Tuskegee University, Rayfield was not satisfied with the few textbooks available. In late 1902, Rayfield prepared this Industrial Drawing Book to be used in his department. The book was used in the introductory course on industrial drawing to give a thorough knowledge of the use of instruments, a few fundamental geometrical problems as an aid in projection, and a short course in simple projection. It was sold for fifty cents a copy. The following is a replication of the original book.

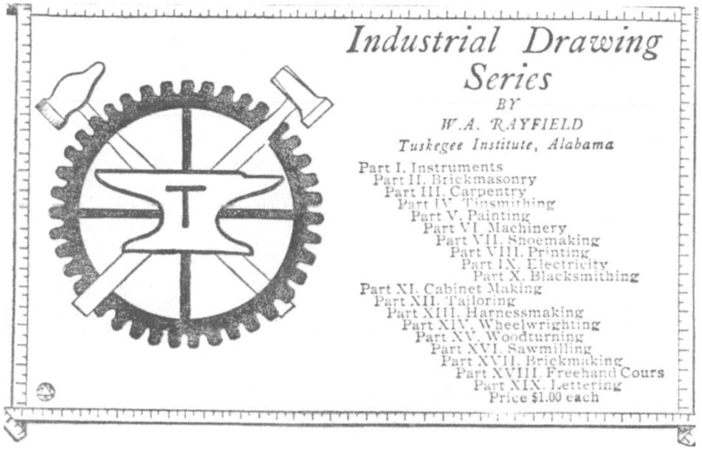

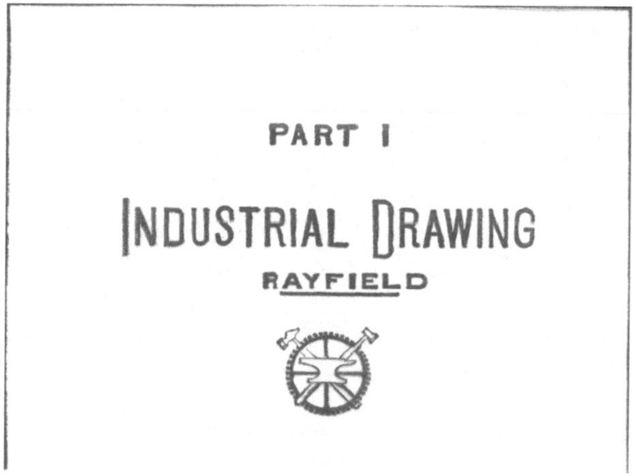

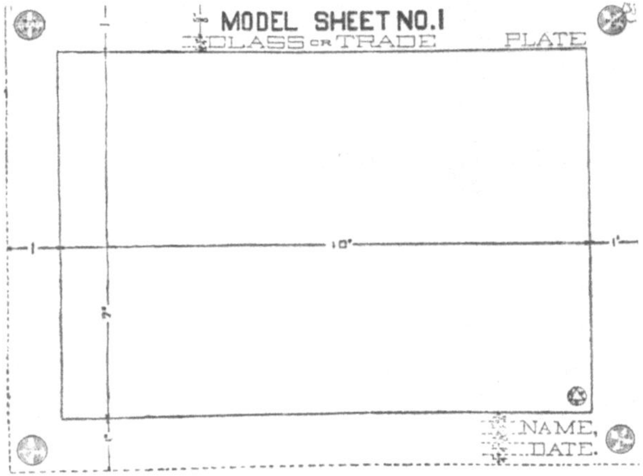
MODEL SHEET NO. 1
CLASS OR TRADE
PLATE
NAME.
DATE.

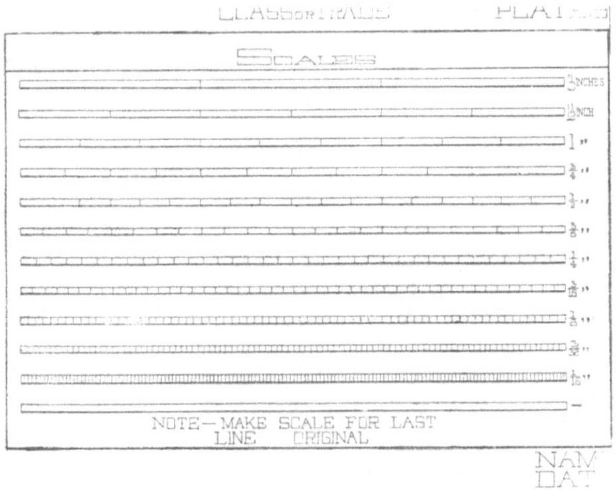
SCALES
NOTE—MAKE SCALE FOR LAST LINE ORIGINAL

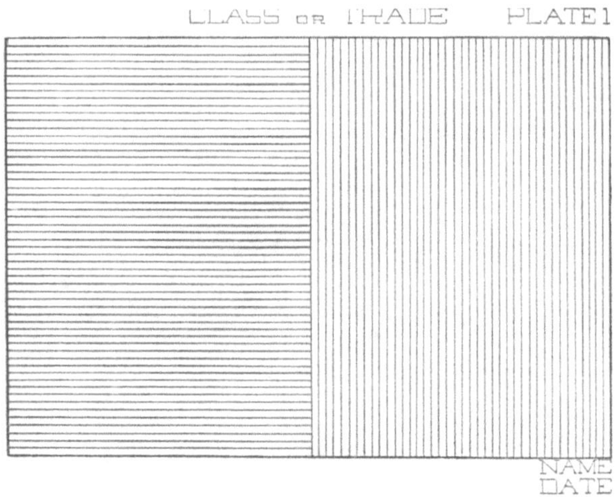
CLASS OR TRADE
PLATE 1
NAME
DATE

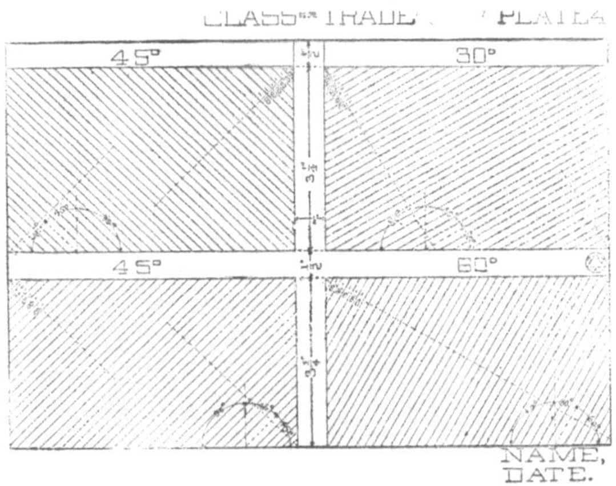
45°
30°
45°
60°
NAME.
DATE.

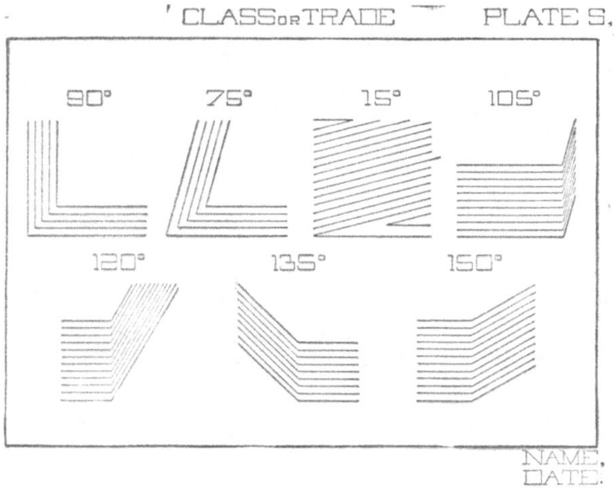
CLASS OR TRADE
PLATE 5.
90°
75°
15°
105°
120°
135°
150°
NAME,
DATE.

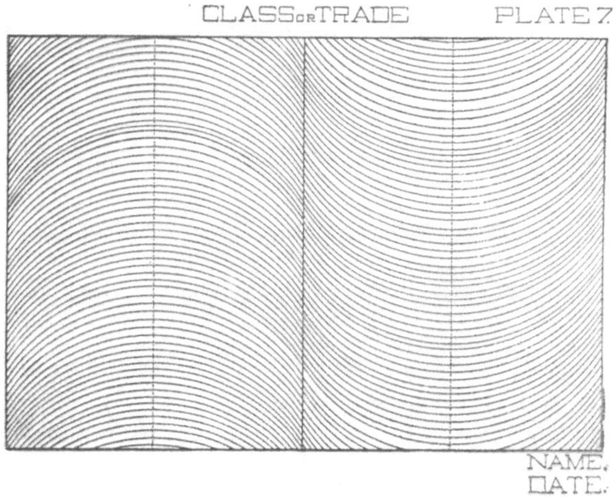
CLASS OR TRADE
PLATE 7.
NAME,
DATE.

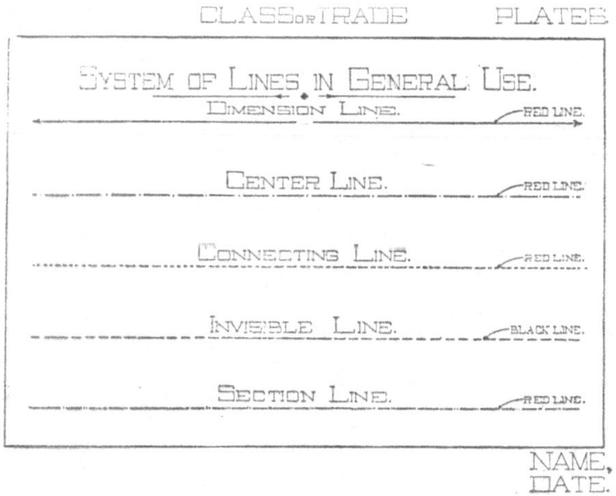
CLASS OR TRADE
PLATE 6
SYSTEM OF LINES IN GENERAL USE.
DIMENSION LINE.
RED LINE.
CENTER LINE.
RED LINE.
CONNECTING LINE.
RED LINE.
INVISIBLE LINE.
BLACK LINE.
SECTION LINE.
RED LINE.
NAME,
DATE.

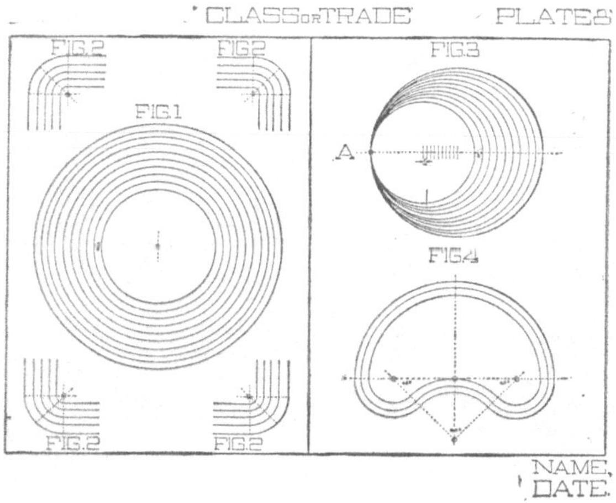
CLASS OR TRADE
PLATE 8
FIG.2
FIG.2
FIG.1
FIG.3
A
FIG.4
FIG.2
FIG.2
NAME,
DATE.

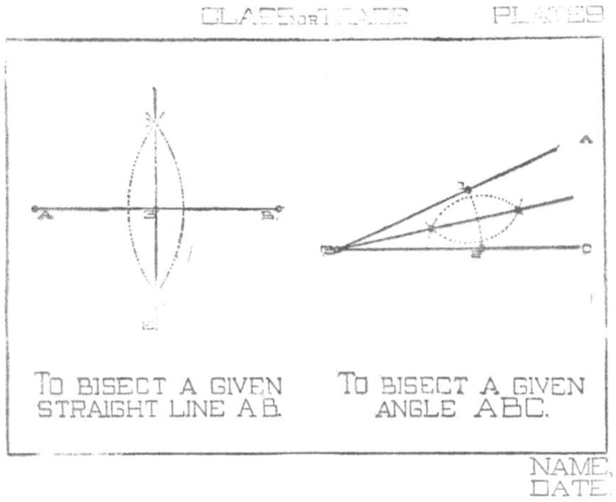
CLASS OR TRADE PLATE 9
A
B
C
D
E
TO BISECT A GIVEN STRAIGHT LINE AB.
TO BISECT A GIVEN ANGLE ABC.
NAME,
DATE.

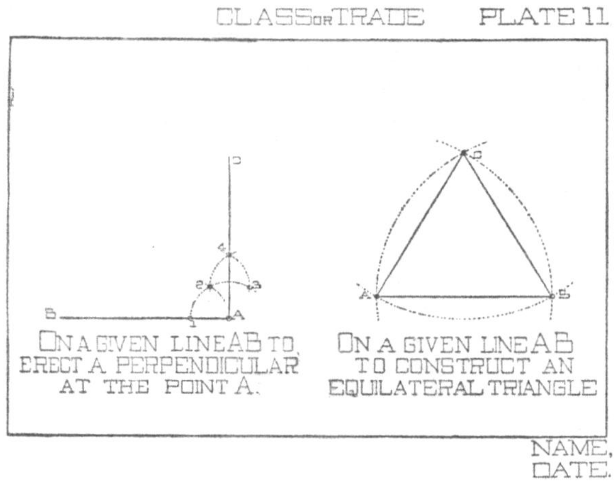
CLASS OR TRADE PLATE 11
ON A GIVEN LINE AB TO ERECT A PERPENDICULAR AT THE POINT A.
ON A GIVEN LINE AB TO CONSTRUCT AN EQUILATERAL TRIANGLE
NAME,
DATE.

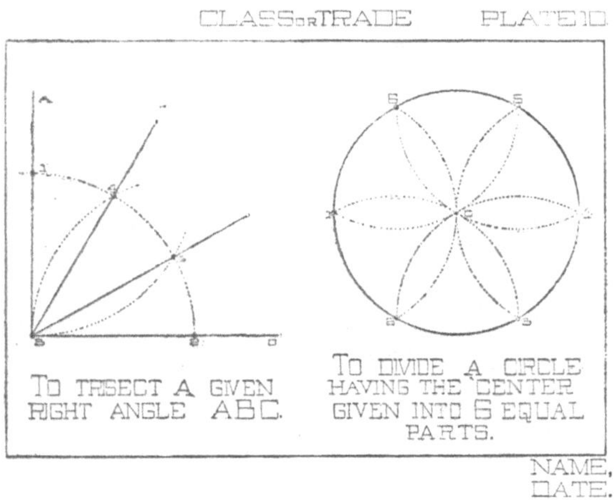
CLASS OR TRADE PLATE 10
TO TRISECT A GIVEN RIGHT ANGLE ABC.
TO DIVIDE A CIRCLE HAVING THE CENTER GIVEN INTO 6 EQUAL PARTS.
NAME,
DATE.

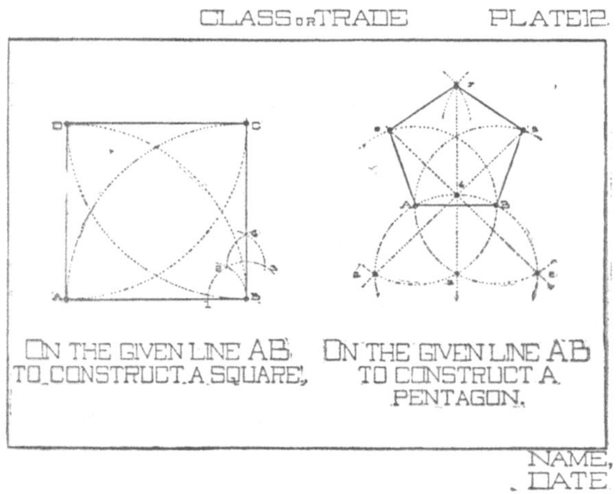
CLASS OR TRADE PLATE 12
ON THE GIVEN LINE AB TO CONSTRUCT A SQUARE.
ON THE GIVEN LINE AB TO CONSTRUCT A PENTAGON.
NAME,
DATE

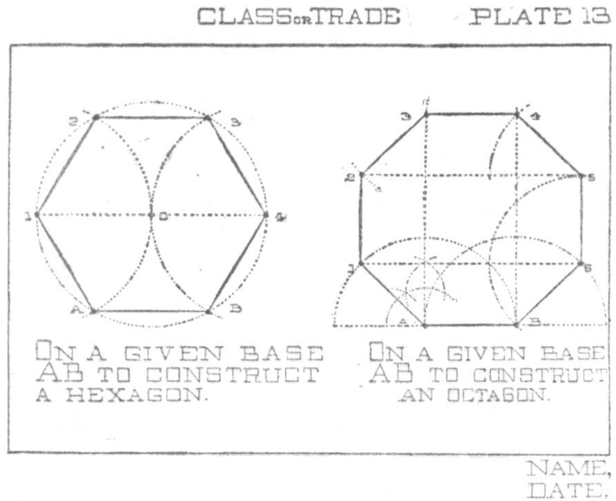
CLASS OR TRADE PLATE 13
ON A GIVEN BASE AB TO CONSTRUCT A HEXAGON.
ON A GIVEN BASE AB TO CONSTRUCT AN OCTAGON.
NAME,
DATE.

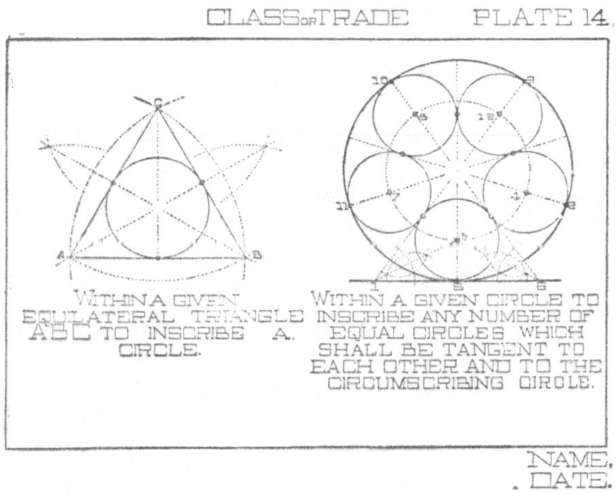
CLASS OR TRADE PLATE 14.
WITHIN A GIVEN EQUILATERAL TRIANGLE ABC TO INSCRIBE A CIRCLE.
WITHIN A GIVEN CIRCLE TO INSCRIBE ANY NUMBER OF EQUAL CIRCLES WHICH SHALL BE TANGENT TO EACH OTHER AND TO THE CIRCUMSCRIBING CIRCLE.
NAME,
DATE.

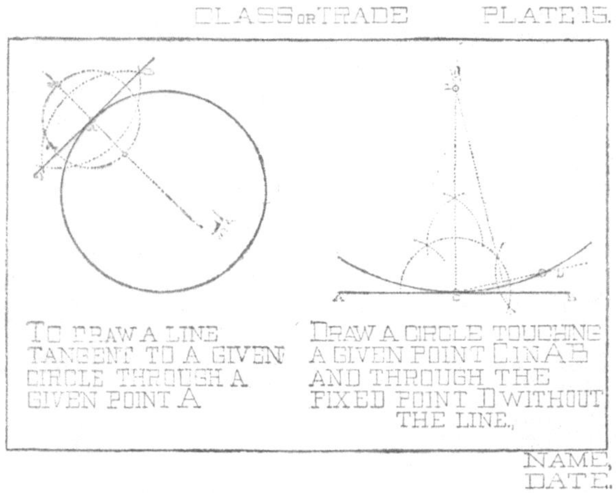
CLASS OR TRADE PLATE 15.
TO DRAW A LINE TANGENT TO A GIVEN CIRCLE THROUGH A GIVEN POINT A
DRAW A CIRCLE TOUCHING A GIVEN POINT C IN AB AND THROUGH THE FIXED POINT D WITHOUT THE LINE.
NAME,
DATE.

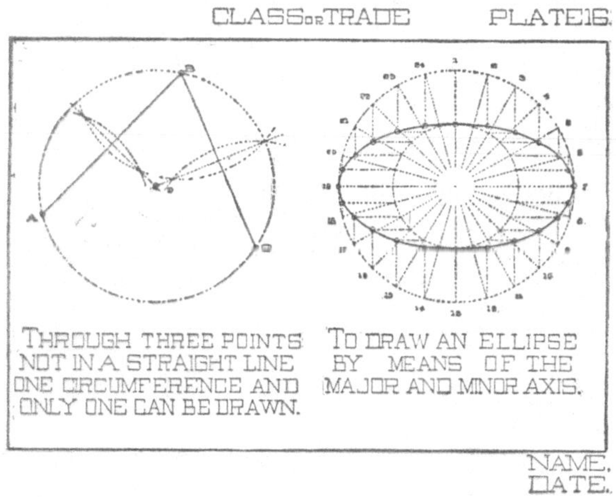
CLASS OR TRADE PLATE 16.
THROUGH THREE POINTS NOT IN A STRAIGHT LINE ONE CIRCUMFERENCE AND ONLY ONE CAN BE DRAWN.
TO DRAW AN ELLIPSE BY MEANS OF THE MAJOR AND MINOR AXIS.
NAME,
DATE.

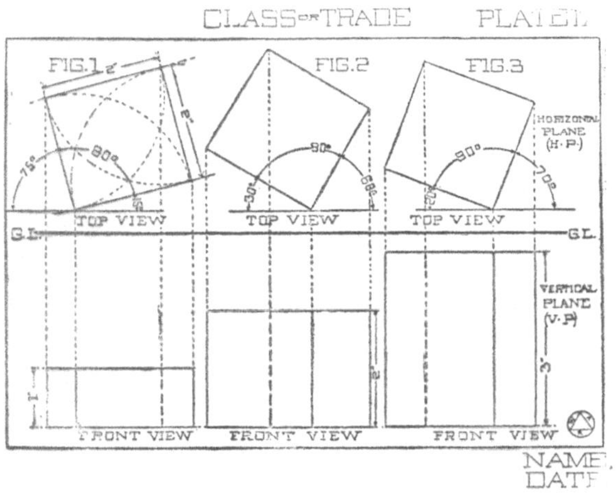
CLASS OR TRADE PLATE 17
FIG. 1
FIG. 2
FIG. 3
HORIZONTAL PLANE (H·P·)
TOP VIEW
TOP VIEW
TOP VIEW
G.L.
G.L.
VERTICAL PLANE (V·P)
FRONT VIEW
FRONT VIEW
FRONT VIEW
NAME,
DATE

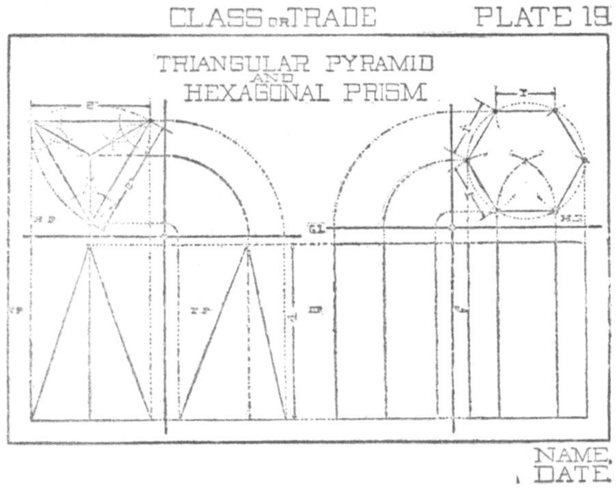
CLASS OR TRADE PLATE 19
TRIANGULAR PYRAMID AND HEXAGONAL PRISM
G.L.
NAME,
DATE

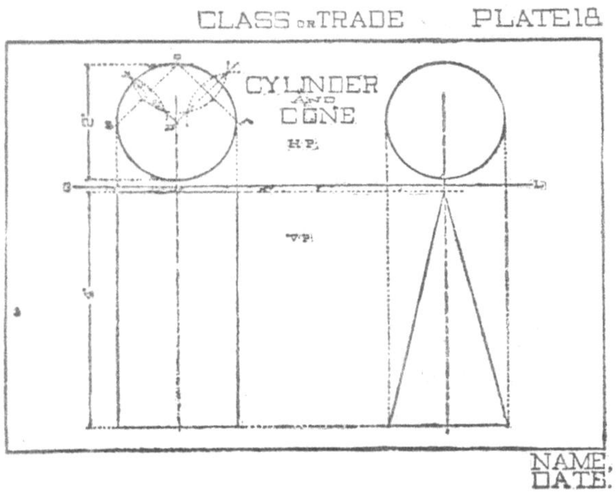
CLASS OR TRADE PLATE 18
CYLINDER AND CONE
H.P.
V.P.
NAME,
DATE.

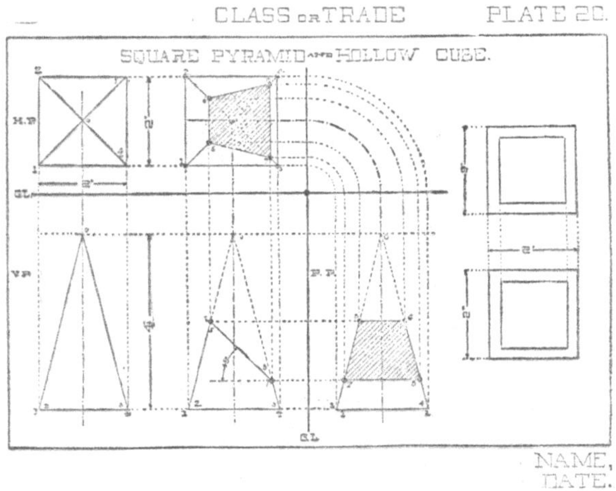
CLASS OR TRADE PLATE 20.
SQUARE PYRAMID AND HOLLOW CUBE.
H.P.
G.L.
V.P.
P.P.
G.L.
NAME,
DATE.

CLASS OR TRADE PLATE 21

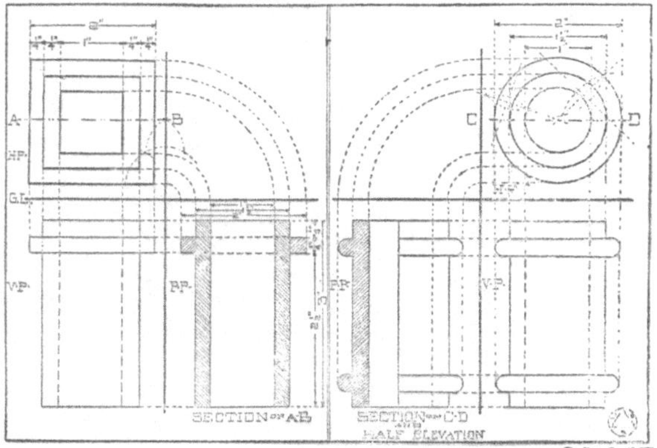

NAME,
DATE.

CLASS OR TRADE PLATE 23.

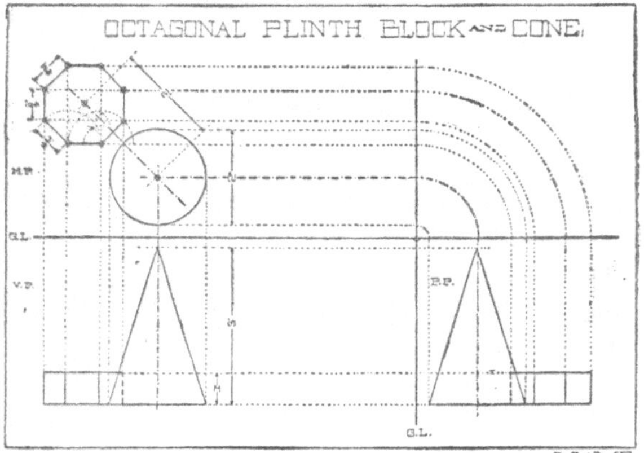

NAME,
DATE.

CLASS OR TRADE PLATE 22.

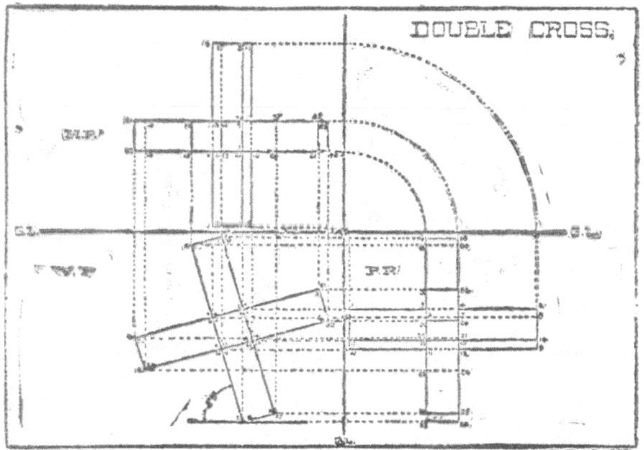

NAME,
DATE.

CLASS OR TRADE PLATE 24.

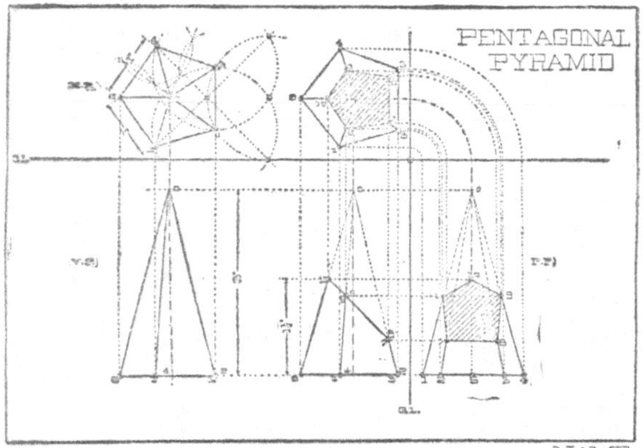

NAME,
DATE.

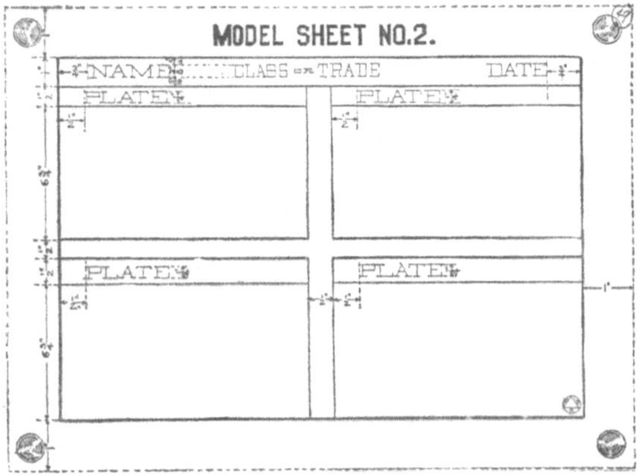
MODEL SHEET NO.2.
NAME
CLASS OR TRADE
DATE
PLATE
PLATE
PLATE
PLATE

LETTERS
ABCDEFGHIJKLMNOPQRSTUVWXYZ
abcdefghijklmnopqrstuvwxyz
AMERICAN EXTRA CONDENSED SERIES
RAPID Fires
STANDARD LINE
Build
Florentine Bold Condensed
RAINS IN NORTH
Lining Quentell No. 2
Brick
KENILWORTH ITALIC
NOBLE TYPE
ABCDEFGHIJKLMNOPQRSTUVWXYZ

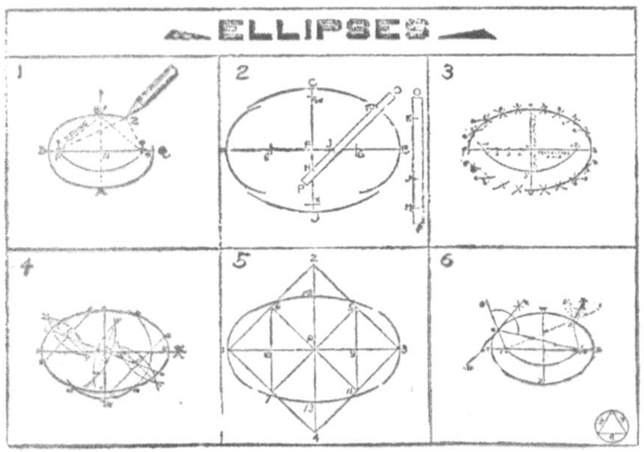
ELLIPSES
1
2
3
4
5
6

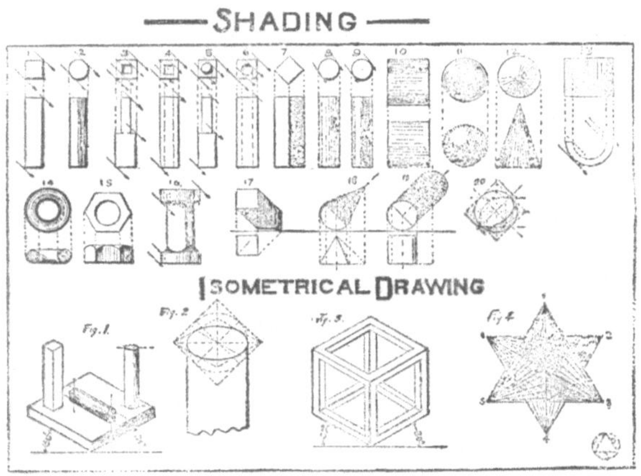
SHADING
ISOMETRICAL DRAWING

— PROJECTION —

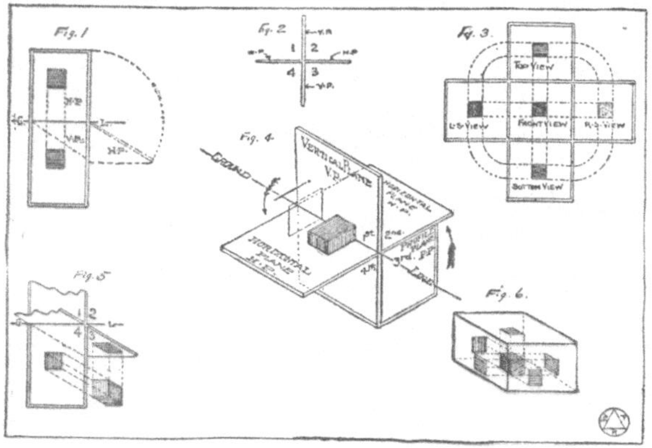

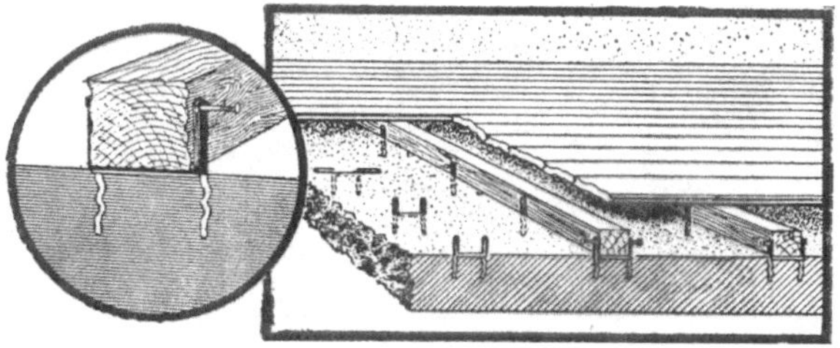

CONVENTIONAL SHEET

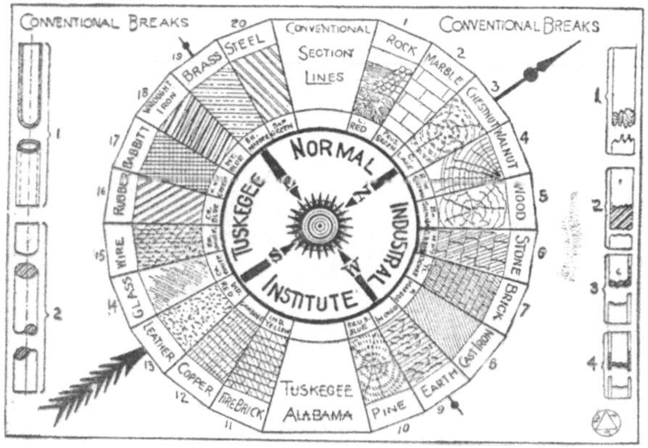

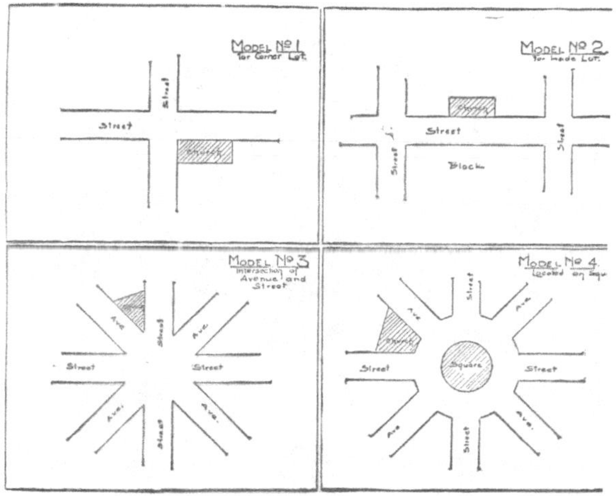

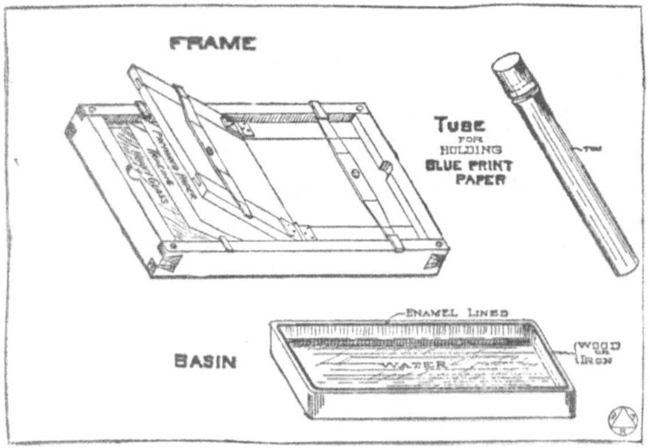
FRAME
TUBE
FOR
HOLDING
BLUE PRINT
PAPER
ENAMEL LINES
BASIN
WATER
WOOD
OR
IRON

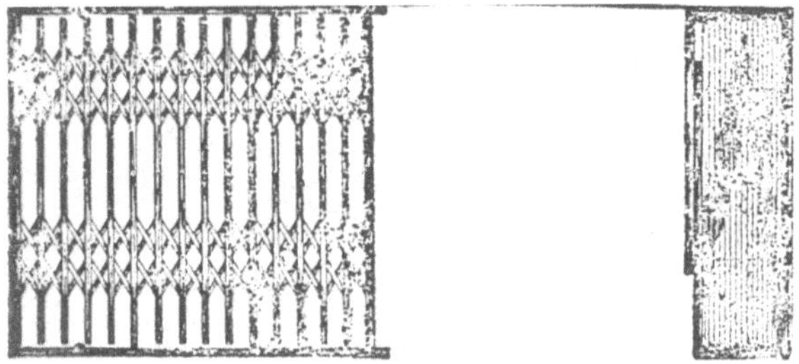

LOVE
FOR
HUMANITY

Bibliography

Alabama Department of Archives and History.

The American Architect. New York: Swetland Publishing. June 19, 1918, 12, 16.

Brown, Charles A. *W. A. Rayfield: Pioneer Black Architect of Birmingham Alabama.* Birmingham: Gray Printing, 1972 (unpublished biography).

"Dr. W. R. Pettiford, the Greatest Banking Genius the Race Has Ever Produced." *Birmingham Reporter.* December 24, 1921, 1.

"Dunbar Hotel." *Birmingham Reporter.* September 11, 1926, 2.

Fort Worth Public Library Web site.

Freedmen's Aid Society.

"Hudson School." *Alabama School Journal* 39, no. 7 (1922): 7.

"Hudson School." *Birmingham Reporter* April 1, 1922, 1.

"Hudson School Is Dedicated by Big Program." *Birmingham Reporter.* September 9, 1922, 1.

Industrial Development and Manufacturers Record. Atlanta: Conway Publications.

"Madam Clisby." *Birmingham Reporter.* October 28, 1922.

Miles College Catalog. Birmingham: Miles College, 1936–37, 11.

"Pythian Temple." *Birmingham Reporter.* January 22, 1921.

"Pythian Temple." *Birmingham Reporter.* June 16, 1921.

Richardson, Clement. *The National Cyclopedia of the Colored Race.* Montgomery: National Publishing, 1919.

Satterfield, Carolyn Green, PhD. *Historic Sites of Jefferson County, Alabama.* Birmingham: Jefferson County Historical Commission, 1976.

Scott, Emett J. "Industrial Drawing." *Tuskegee Student.* October 15, 1904.

Index

Page numbers in italics refer to illustrations.